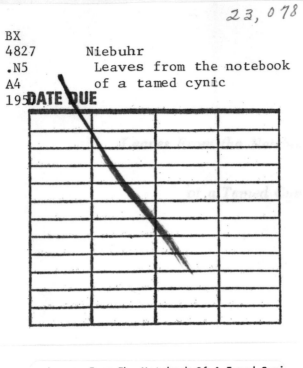

To
my friends
and former co-workers
in
Bethel Evangelical Church
Detroit, Michigan

Stanley Graham

LEAVES

FROM THE NOTEBOOK

OF A TAMED CYNIC

by REINHOLD NIEBUHR

Meridian Books

THE WORLD PUBLISHING COMPANY

CLEVELAND AND NEW YORK

A LIVING AGE BOOK (MERIDIAN)
Published by The World Publishing Company
2231 West 110th Street, Cleveland, Ohio 44102
First Meridian printing July 1957
Seventh Printing November 1966
Copyright © 1929 by Reinhold Niebuhr
Library of Congress Catalog Card Number: 57-10846
Printed in the United States of America   7FD 1166

PREFACE

1956

An author is naturally embarrassed to have a book, first published more than a quarter century ago, re-issued and presumably reaching some new readers who will be astounded by the dated character of the observations in the book. My own embarrassment is the more acute because these autobiographical notes are more than ordinarily dated. They were prompted by the experiences of a young minister serving his first parish in the growing city of Detroit. Some of the observations may have a faint historical significance inasfar as they throw light upon the social climate of a large urban center, the seat of the growing automobile industry in a day in which the unions, which now dominate the picture, were still unheard of.

But the notes are not primarily a social document. As the self-revelations of a young parson they freely express the then typical notions of liberal Protestantism before the whole liberal world view was challenged by world events. Of course they were written after the first world war. But that war did not essentially challenge the liberal culture of America. It required a depression and another world war to corrode an optimism in America which was lost in Europe after the first world war. There are some indications in these notes of uneasiness about the general religious presuppositions which informed a youthful ministry. But on the whole there are no serious evidences of a revolt which occurred in the soul of the author and of many of his contemporaries, only a few years after the book was published. Thus indisputable evidence is offered for the fact that we are all, whatever our pretensions, the children of our day and hour. What we think of man and God, of sin and salvation, is partly prompted by the comparative comforts or discomforts in which we live. It is a very sobering reflection on the lack of transcendence of the human spirit over the flux of historical change.

Perhaps too much has been said about the

embarrassment of the author because of the "dated" character of his views. The notes are primarily a record of the experiences of a young minister and they will have interest primarily to other young ministers. I have no embarrassment about the fact that the notes reveal the satisfaction which one may have in preaching the gospel and "tending the flock" in a local parish. And I hope that they may also reveal some of the variegated problems and issues which confront the Christian ministry. After a quarter of a century in academic life, I can still understand why I was so reluctant to leave the local parish. Academic life seems highly specialized in comparison with the life of a parish priest meeting human problems on all levels of weal and woe, and trying to be helpful in fashioning a "community of grace" in the barren anonymity of a large city.

I regret the immaturity with which I approached the problems and tasks of the ministry but I do not regret the years devoted to the parish.

REINHOLD NIEBUHR

PREFACE AND APOLOGY

Most of the reflections recorded in these pages were prompted by experiences of a local Christian pastorate. Some are derived from wider contacts with the churches and colleges of the country. For the sake of giving a better clue to the meaning of a few of them, it may be necessary to say that they have as their background a pastorate in an industrial community in which the natural growth of the city made the expansion of a small church into a congregation of considerable size, in a period of thirteen years, inevitable. By the time these lines reach the reader the author will have exchanged his pastoral activities for academic pursuits.

It must be confessed in all candor that some of the notes, particularly the later ones, were written after it seemed fairly certain that they would reach the eye of the public in some form or other. It was therefore psychologically difficult to maintain the type of honesty which characterizes the self-revelations of a private diary. The reader must consequently be warned (though such a warning may be superfluous) to discount the unconscious insincerities which no amount of self-discipline can eliminate from words which are meant for the public.

The notes which have been chosen for publication have been picked to illustrate the typical problems of a modern minister in an industrial and urban community and what seem to be more or less typical reactions of a young minister to such problems. Nothing new or startling was attempted in the pastorate out of which these reflections grew. If there is any justification for their publication, it must lie in the light they may throw upon the problems of the modern church and ministry rather than upon any possible solutions of these problems.

The book is published with an uneasy conscience, the author half hoping that the publishers would make short shrift of his indiscretions by throttling the book. Some of the notes are really too inane to deserve inclusion in any published work, and they can be justified only as a background for those notes which deal critically with the problems of the modern ministry. The latter are unfortunately, in many instances, too impertinent to be in good taste, and I lacked the grace to rob them of their impertinence without destroying whatever critical value they might possess. I can only emphasize in extenuation of the spirit which prompted them, what is confessed in some of the criticisms, namely, that the author is not unconscious of what the critical reader will himself divine, a tendency to be most critical of that in other men to which he is most tempted himself.

The modern ministry is in no easy position; for it is committed to the espousal of ideals (professionally, at that) which are in direct conflict with the dominant interests and prejudices of contemporary civilization. This conflict is nowhere more apparent than in America, where neither ancient sanctities nor new social insights tend to qualify, as they do in Europe, the heedless economic forces of an industrial era.

Inevitably a compromise must be made, or is made, between the rigor of the ideal and the necessities of the day. That has always been the case, but the resulting compromises are more obvious to an astute observer in our own day than in other generations. We are a world-conscious generation, and we have the means at our disposal to see and to analyze the brutalities which characterize men's larger social relationships and to note the dehumanizing effects of a civilization which unites men mechanically and isolates them spiritually.

Our knowledge may ultimately be the means of our redemption, but for the moment it seems to rob us of self-respect and respect for one another. Every conscientious minister is easily tempted to a sense of futility because we live our lives microscopically while we are able to view the scene in which we labor telescopically. But the higher perspective has its advantages as well as its dangers. It saves us from too much self-deception. Men who are engaged in the espousal of ideals easily fall into sentimentality. From the outside and the disinterested perspective this sentimentality may seem like hypocrisy. If it is only sentimentality and self-deception, viewed at closer range, it may degenerate into real hypocrisy if no determined effort is made to reduce it to a minimum.

It is no easy task to deal realistically with the moral confusion of our day, either in the pulpit or the pew, and avoid the appearance, and possibly the actual peril, of cynicism. An age which obscures the essentially unethical nature of its dominant interests by an undue preoccupation with the application of Christian principles in limited areas, may, as a matter of fact, deserve and profit by ruthless satire. Yet the pedagogical merits of satire are dubious, and in any event its weapons will be foresworn by an inside critic for both selfish and social reasons. For reasons of self-defense he will be very gentle in dealing with limitations which his own life illustrates.

But he will be generous in judgment for another reason. His intimate view of the facts will help him to see that what an outside critic may call hyprocrisy may really be honest, because of its unconscious sentimentality and self-deception. When virtues are used to hide moral limitations the critic ought not to be too sure that the virtues are bogus. Sometimes they are. But sometimes they merely represent the effort of honest but short-sighted men to preserve the excellencies of another day long after these have ceased to have relevancy for the problems of our own day; or sometimes they spring from efforts to apply the Christian ideal to limited and immediate areas of conduct where application is fairly easy. In such cases no one can be absolutely sure whether it is want of perspective or want of courage which hinders the Christian idealist from applying his ideals and principles to the more remote and the more difficult relationships.

That the ministry is particularly tempted to the self-deceptions which afflict the moral life of Christians today is obvious. If it is dangerous to entertain great moral ideals without attempting to realize them in life, it is even more perilous to proclaim them in abstract terms without bringing them into juxtaposition with the specific social and moral issues of the day. The minister's premature satisfaction in the presentation of moral ideals is accentuated by the fact that he is a leader in a community in which appreciative attitudes are on the whole more prevalent than critical ones. The minister is therefore easily fooled by extravagant conceptions of his own moral stature, held by admiring parishioners. If he could realize how much of this appreciation represents transferred religious emotion he could be more realistic in analyzing himself. And if he could persuade himself to speak of moral ideals in terms of specific issues and contemporary situations, he would probably prompt currents of critical thought which would destroy the aura which invests his person with premature sanctity.

If a minister wants to be a man among men he need only to stop creating devotion to abstract ideals which every one accepts in theory and denies in practice, and to agonize about their validity and practicability in the social issues which he and others face in our present civilization. That immediately gives his ministry a touch of reality and potency and robs it of an artificial prestige which it can afford to dispense with, and is bound to be stripped of, the kind of prestige which is the prerogative of priests and professional holy men.

The number of ministers who are perfectly realistic about their tasks and who are sincerely anxious to help the modern generation find itself, not only in the intricate problems of the personal life but in the moral and social complexities of an industrial society, is much larger than the critics outside of the church are able to know and willing to concede. If I have any regrets, it is that these pages, preoccupied with criticism, deal inadequately with such men and fail to discharge my debt of gratitude to them. It is comparatively easy for professors, secretaries and even bishops to criticize the man in a local situation from the perspective and the safety (relative, of course,) which an irresponsible itinerancy supplies.

No amount of pressure from an itinerant "prophet" can change the fact that a minister is bound to be a statesman as much as a prophet, dealing with situations as well as principles. In specific situations, actions must be judged not only in terms of absolute standards but in consideration of available resources in the lives of those whom the minister leads.

It may be well for the statesman to know that statesmanship easily degenerates into opportunism and that opportunism cannot be sharply distinguished from dishonesty. But the prophet ought to realize that his higher perspective and the uncompromising nature of his judgments always has a note of irresponsibility in it. Francis of Assisi may have been a better Christian than Pope Innocent III. But it may be questioned whether his moral superiority over the latter was as absolute as it seemed. Nor is there any reason to believe that Abraham Lincoln, the statesman and opportunist, was morally inferior to William Lloyd Garrison, the prophet. The moral achievement of statesmen must be judged in terms which take account of the limitations of human society which the statesman must, and the prophet need not, consider.

Having both entered and left the parish ministry against my inclinations, I pay my tribute to the calling, firm in the conviction that it offers greater opportunities for both moral adventure and social usefulness than any other calling if it is entered with open eyes and a consciousness of the hazards to virtue which lurk in it. I make no apology for being critical of what I love. No one wants a love which is based upon illusions, and there is no reason why we should not love a profession and yet be critical of it.

REINHOLD NIEBUHR

LEAVES FROM THE NOTEBOOK OF A TAMED CYNIC

1915

There is something ludicrous about a callow young fool like myself standing up to preach a sermon to these good folks. I talk wisely about life and know little about life's problems. I tell them of the need of sacrifice, although most of them could tell me something about what that really means. I preached a sermon the other day on "The Involuntary Cross," using the text of Simon the Cyrene bearing the cross of Jesus. A good woman, a little bolder than the rest, asked me in going out whether I had borne many crosses. I think I know a little more about that than I would be willing to confess to her or to the congregation, but her question was justified.

Many of the people insist that they can't understand how a man so young as I could possibly be a preacher. Since I am twenty-three their reaction to my youth simply means that they find something incompatible even between the ripe age of twenty-three and the kind of seasoned wisdom which they expect from the pulpit. "Let no one despise thy youth," said Paul to Timothy; but I doubt whether that advice stopped any of the old saints from wagging their heads. I found it hard the first few months to wear a pulpit gown. Now I am getting accustomed to it. At first I felt too much like a priest in it, and I abhor priestliness. I have become reconciled to it partly as a simple matter of habit, but I imagine that I am also beginning to like the gown as a kind of symbol of authority. It gives me the feeling that I am speaking not altogether in my own name and out of my own experience but by the authority of the experience of many Christian centuries.

Difficult as the pulpit job is, it is easier than the work in the organizations of the congregation. Where did anyone ever learn in a seminary how to conduct or help with a Ladies Aid meeting? I am glad that mother has come to live with me and will take care of that part of the job. It is easier to speak sagely from the pulpit than to act wisely in the detailed tasks of the parish. A young preacher would do well to be heard more than he is seen.

1915

I am glad there are only eighteen families in this church. I have been visiting the members for six weeks and haven't seen all of them yet. Usually I walk past a house two or three times before I summon the courage to go in. I am always very courteously received, so I don't know exactly why I should not be able to overcome this curious timidity. I don't know that very much comes of my visits except that I really get acquainted with the people.

Usually after I have made a call I find some good excuse to quit for the afternoon. I used to do that in the days gone by when I was a book agent. But there was reason for it then. I needed the afternoon to regain my self-respect. Now it seems to be pure laziness and fear. The people are a little discouraged. Some of them seem to doubt whether the church will survive. But there are a few who are the salt of the earth, and if I make a go of this they will be more responsible than they will ever know.

1915

Now that I have preached about a dozen sermons I find I am repeating myself. A different
text simply means a different pretext for saying
the same thing over again. The few ideas that
I had worked into sermons at the seminary have
all been used, and now what? I suppose that as
the years go by life and experience will prompt
some new ideas and I will find some in the Bible
that I have missed so far. They say a young
preacher must catch his second wind before he
can really preach. I'd better catch it pretty soon
or the weekly sermon will become a terrible
chore.

You are supposed to stand before a congregation, brimming over with a great message.
Here I am trying to find a new little message
each Sunday. If I really had great convictions
I suppose they would struggle for birth each
week. As the matter stands, I struggle to find
an idea worth presenting and I almost dread
the approach of a new sabbath. I don't know
whether I can ever accustom myself to the task
of bringing light and inspiration in regular
weekly installments.

How in the world can you reconcile the inevitability of Sunday and its tasks with the moods and caprices of the soul? The prophet speaks only when he is inspired. The parish preacher must speak whether he is inspired or not. I wonder whether it is possible to live on a high enough plane to do that without sinning against the Holy Spirit.

1916

Visited old Mrs. G. today and gave her communion. This was my first experience with communion at the sick bed. I think there is a good deal of superstition connected with the rite. It isn't very much different in some of its aspects from the Catholic rite of extreme unction. Yet I will not be too critical. If the rite suggests and expresses the emotion of honest contrition it is more than superstition. But that is the difficulty of acting as priest. It is not in your power to determine the use of a symbol. Whether it is a blessing or a bit of superstition rests altogether with the recipient.

I must admit that I am losing some of the aversion to the sacraments cultivated in my seminary days. There is something very beautiful about parents bringing their child to the altar with a prayer of thanksgiving and as an act of dedication. The trouble is that the old ritual in the book of forms does not express this idea clearly. I have to put the whole meaning of the sacrament as I see it into the prayer. Perhaps I can use my own form later on, if I get the confidence of the people.

Incidentally Mrs. G. gave me a shock this afternoon. After the service was completed she fished around under her pillow and brought forth a five dollar bill. That was to pay me for my trouble. I never knew this fee business still existed in such a form in Protestantism. I knew they were still paying for baptism in some denominations, ours included. But this is a new one. The old lady was a little hurt, I think, by my refusal. I think she imagined that pity prompted my diffidence. She insisted that she was quite able to pay. I'd better get started on this whole fee question and make an announcement that I won't accept any fees for anything. I think I'll except weddings however. Every one takes fees for them. It will just make a scene when the groom or best man slyly crosses your palm with a bill and you make a righteous refusal. They never will understand. Marriage is not a sacrament anyway. Then, too, it's fun getting a little extra money once in a while. But isn't marriage a sacrament?

1916

Doesn't this denominational business wear on one's nerves? If I were a doctor people would consult me according to the skill I had and the reputation I could acquire. But being a minister I can appeal only to people who are labeled as I am. Yesterday that professor I met asked me what denomination I belonged to. Being told, he promptly pigeonholed me into my proper place and with a superior air assumed that my mind was as definitely set by my denominational background as is that of an African Hottentot by his peculiar environment.

Perhaps if I belonged to a larger denomination this wouldn't irk me so much. I suffer from an inferiority complex because of the very numerical weakness of my denomination. If I belonged to a large one I might strut about and claim its glory for myself. If I give myself to religion as a profession I must find some interdenominational outlet for my activities. But what? Secretaries and Y.M.C.A. workers are too inarticulate. They deal too much with machinery and too little with ideas. I don't want to be a chauffeur. Does that mean that I am a minister merely because I am a fairly glib talker? Who knows?

But let us not be too cynical and too morbidly introspective. I may find something worth saying in time and escape the fate of being a mere talker. At any rate I swear that I will never aspire to be a preacher of pretty sermons. I'll keep them rough just to escape the temptation of degenerating into an elocutionist. Maybe I had better stop quoting so much poetry. But that is hardly the point. Plenty of sermons lack both beauty and meaning.

1916

The young fellows I am trying to teach in Sunday school don't listen to me attentively. I don't think I am getting very close to where they live. Or perhaps I just haven't learned how to put my message across. I am constantly interrupted in my talk by the necessity of calling someone to order. It is a good thing that I have a class like that. I'll venture that my sermons aren't getting any nearer to the people, but the little group of adults I am speaking to in the morning service are naturally more patient or at least more polite than these honest youngsters, and so I have less chance to find out from them how futile I am. But that doesn't solve the problem of how to reach those fellows.

1916

I had a letter from Professor L—— today suggesting that I return to college and prepare myself for the teaching profession. A year ago I was certain that I would do that. Now I am not so sure. Nevertheless the academic life has its allurements. It is really simpler than the ministry. As a teacher your only task is to discover the truth. As a preacher you must conserve other interests besides the truth. It is your business to deal circumspectly with the whole religious inheritance lest the virtues which are involved in the older traditions perish through your iconoclasm. That is a formidable task and a harassing one; for one can never be quite sure where pedagogical caution ends and dishonesty begins.

What is particularly disquieting to a young man in the ministry is the fact that some of his fine old colleagues make such a virtue of their ignorance. They are sure that there is no Second Isaiah and have never heard that Deuteronomy represents a later development in the law. I can't blame them for not having all the bright new knowledge of a recent seminarian (not quite as new as the seminarian imagines); but the ministry is the only profession in which you can make a virtue of ignorance. If you have read nothing but commentaries for twenty years, that is supposed to invest you with an aura of sanctity and piety. Every profession has its traditions and its traditionalists. But the traditionalists in the pulpit are much more certain than the others that the Lord is on their side.

1917

Next week we are going to hold our first every member canvass. They expect me to preach a sermon which will prepare the good people to give generously. I don't mind that. Most people give little enough for the church or for anything else not connected with their own pleasures. But I don't see how you can preach a sermon adequate to the needs of the moment without identifying the church with the kingdom of God too unqualifiedly. And meanwhile you are drawing your salary from the church and remembering that if the canvass is a success there may be an increase in salary next year. It isn't easy to mix the business of preaching with the business of making a living and maintain your honesty and self-respect.

Of course every laborer is worthy of his hire. But you notice that Paul, who insisted on that point, nevertheless prided himself on his independence. He wanted "not yours but you." But let us not be too squeamish. There is old J.Q. It would do his soul good if he loosened up a bit. One might say to him, "I want yours so that I can get you."

1918

(After a trip through the war training camps.)

I hardly know how to bring order out of confusion in my mind in regard to this war. I think that if Wilson's aims are realized the war will serve a good purpose. When I talk to the boys I make much of the Wilsonian program as against the kind of diplomacy which brought on the war. But it is easier to talk about the aims of the war than to justify its methods.

Out at Funston I watched a bayonet practice. It was enough to make me feel like a brazen hypocrite for being in this thing, even in a rather indirect way. Yet I cannot bring myself to associate with the pacifists. Perhaps if I were not of German blood I could. That may be cowardly, but I do think that a new nation has a right to be pretty sensitive about its unity.

Some of the good old Germans have a hard time hiding a sentiment which borders very closely on hatred for this nation. Anyone who dissociates himself from the cause of his nation in such a time as this ought to do it only on the basis of an unmistakably higher loyalty. If I

dissociated myself only slightly I would inevitably be forced into the camp of those who
romanticize about the Kaiser. And the Kaiser
is certainly nothing to me. If we must have war
I'll certainly feel better on the side of Wilson
than on the side of the Kaiser.

What makes me angry is the way I kowtow
to the chaplains as I visit the various camps.
Here are ministers of the gospel just as I am.
Just as I they are also, for the moment, priests
of the great god Mars. As ministers of the Christian religion I have no particular respect for
them. Yet I am overcome by a terrible inferiority
complex when I deal with them. Such is the
power of a uniform. Like myself, they have
mixed the worship of the God of love and the
God of battles. But unlike myself, they have
adequate symbols of this double devotion. The
little cross on the shoulder is the symbol of their
Christian faith. The uniform itself is the symbol
of their devotion to the God of battles. It is the
uniform and not the cross which impresses me
and others. I am impressed even when I know
that I ought not be.

What I dislike about most of the chaplains
is that they assume a very officious and also a
very masculine attitude. Ministers are not used
to authority and revel in it when acquired. The
rather too obvious masculinity which they try

to suggest by word and action is meant to re-
move any possible taint which their Christian
faith might be suspected to have left upon them
in the minds of the he-men in the army. H——
is right. He tells me that he wants to go into
the army as a private and not as a chaplain. He
believes that the war is inevitable but he is not
inclined to reconcile its necessities with the
Christian ethic. He will merely forget about this
difficulty during the war. That is much more
honest than what I am doing.

1918

I can see one element in this strange fascination of war which men have not adequately noted. It reduces life to simple terms. The modern man lives in such a complex world that one wonders how his sanity is maintained as well as it is. Every moral venture, every social situation and every practical problem involves a whole series of conflicting loyalties, and a man may never be quite sure that he is right in giving himself to the one as against the other. Shall he be just and sacrifice love? Shall he strive for beauty and do it by gaining the social privileges which destroy his sense of fellowship with the under-privileged? Shall he serve his family and neglect the state? Or be patriotic to the detriment of the great family of mankind? Shall he be diligent at the expense of his health? Or keep healthy at the expense of the great cause in which he is interested? Shall he be truthful and therefore cruel? Or shall he be kind and therefore a little soft? Shall he strive for the amenities of life and make life less robust in the process? Or shall he make courage the ultimate virtue and brush aside the virtues which a stable and therefore soft society has cultivated?

Out of this mesh of conflicting claims, interests, loyalties, ideals, values and communities he is rescued by the psychology of war which gives the state at least a momentary priority over all other communities and which makes courage the supreme virtue. I talked to a young captain at camp last week who told me how happy he was in the army because he had "found himself" in military service. Our further conversation led me to suspect that it was this simplification of life which had really brought him happiness; that and his love of authority.

Unfortunately, all these momentary simplifications of the complexities of life cannot be finally satisfying, because they do violence to life. The imperiled community may for a moment claim a kind of unqualified loyalty which no community or cause has the right or ability to secure in normal times. But judgment returns to sobriety as events become less disjointed and the world is once more revealed in all its confusion of good in evil and evil in good. The imperiled community was threatened because of its vice as much as because of its virtue, and the diabolical foe reassumes the lineaments of our common humanity. Physical courage is proved unequal to the task of ennobling man without the aid of other virtues, and the same men who have been raised to great heights by the self-forgetfulness of war have been sunk into new depths of hatred. There is only momentary peace in an all-consuming passion, except it be a passion for what is indubitably the best. And what is the best?

1919

We had a great Easter service today. Mother made the little chapel look very pretty, working with a committee of young women. It takes real work to decorate such a little place, and make it really inviting. We received our largest class of new members into the church thus far, twenty-one in all. Most of them had no letters from other churches and yet had been reared in some church. We received them on reaffirmation of faith.

This matter of recruiting a membership for the church is a real problem. Even the churches which once believed a very definite conversion to be the sine qua non of entrance into the fellowship of the church are going in for "decision days" as they lose confidence in the traditional assumption that one can become a Christian only through a crisis experience. But if one does not insist on that kind of an experience it is not so easy to set up tests of membership. Most of these "personal evangelism" campaigns mean little more than an ordinary recruiting effort with church membership rather than the Christian life as the real objective.

They do not differ greatly from efforts of various clubs as they seek to expand their membership.

Of course we make "acceptance of Jesus as your savior" the real door into the fellowship of the church. But the trouble is that this may mean everything or nothing. I see no way of making the Christian fellowship unique by any series of tests which precede admission. The only possibility lies in a winnowing process through the instrumentality of the preaching and teaching function of the church. Let them come in without great difficulty, but make it difficult for them to stay in. The trouble with this plan is that it is always easy to load up your membership with very immature Christians who will finally set the standard and make it impossible to preach and to teach the gospel in its full implications.

1919

What a picture that is of Wilson, Lloyd George
and Clemenceau settling the fate of the world
in Paris! Wilson is evidently losing his battle.
He would have done better to stay at home and
throw bolts from Olympus. If you have honest
and important differences of opinion with others,
it is better to write letters than to put your feet
under the same table with them. Compromises
are always more inevitable in personal contact
than in long distance negotiation.

What seems to be happening at Paris is that
they will let Wilson label the transaction if the
others can determine its true import. Thus realities are exchanged for words. There will be "no
indemnities" but of course there will be reparations; and, since the damage was great, the
reparations may be made larger than any so-
called indemnity of the past. There will be "no
annexations" but there will be mandates.

Wilson is a typical son of the manse. He believes too much in words. The sly Clemenceau
sneaks new meanings into these nice words, in
which task he is probably ably helped by Mr.
Lloyd George, who is an admirable go-between,

being as worldly wise as M. Clemenceau and as evangelical as Mr. Wilson. Yet who knows? Time may yet give Mr. Wilson the victory. Words have certain meanings of which it is hard to rob them, and ideas may create reality in time. The league of nations may be, for the time being, merely a league of victors but it will be difficult to destroy the redemptive idea at the heart of it completely. Realities are always defeating ideals, but ideals have a way of taking vengeance upon the facts which momentarily imprison them.

On the other hand, it is always possible that diabolical facts will so discredit the idea which they ostensibly incarnate that they will necessitate the projection of a new idea before progress can be made.

1919

Visited Miss Z. at the hospital. I like to go now since she told me that it helps her to have me pray with her. I asked the doctor about her and he says her case is hopeless. Here faith seems really to be functioning in lifting the soul above physical circumstance. I have been so afraid of quackery that I have leaned over backwards trying to avoid the encouragement of false hopes. Sometimes when I compare myself with these efficient doctors and nurses hustling about I feel like an ancient medicine man dumped into the twentieth century. I think they have about the same feeling toward me that I have about myself.

It must be very satisfying to deal as an exact scientist with known data upon which to base your conclusions. I have to work in the twilight zone where superstition is inextricably mixed up with something that is—well, not superstition. I do believe that Jesus healed people. I can't help but note, however, that a large proportion of his cures were among the demented. If people ask me, I tell them that religion has more therapeutic value in functional than in organic diseases. But I don't know whether I am altogether honest about this at the bedside. I am still praying for health with Miss Z. But of course I don't leave it at that. I am trying to prepare her for the inevitable and I think I have helped her a little in that respect.

1919

This sickness of Miss Z.'s is getting on my nerves. I can't think of anything for the rest of the day after coming from that bed of pain. If I had more patients I suppose I would get a little more hardened. Talk about professionalism! I suppose men get professional to save their emotional resources. Here I make one visit in an afternoon and get all done up. Meanwhile the doctor is making a dozen. He is less sentimental, but probably does more good.

1920

I am really beginning to like the ministry. I
think since I have stopped worrying so much
about the intellectual problems of religion and
have begun to explore some of its ethical problems there is more of a thrill in preaching. The
real meaning of the gospel is in conflict with
most of the customs and attitudes of our day at
so many places that there is adventure in the
Christian message, even if you only play around
with its ideas in a conventional world. I can't
say that I have done anything in my life to
dramatize the conflict between the gospel and
the world. But I find it increasingly interesting
to set the two in juxtaposition at least in my
mind and in the minds of others. And of course
ideas may finally lead to action.

A young woman came to me the other day in
—— and told me that my talk on forgiveness in
the C—— Church of that town several months
ago has brought about a reconciliation between
her mother and sister after the two had been in
a feud for five years. I accepted the news with
more outward than inward composure. There is
redemptive power in the message! I could go on

the new courage that came out of that little victory for many a month.

I think I am beginning to like the ministry also because it gives you a splendid opportunity to have all kinds of contacts with people in relationships in which they are at their best. You do get tired of human pettiness at times. But there is nevertheless something quite glorious about folks. That is particularly true when you find them bearing sorrow with real patience. Think of Mrs.—— putting up with that drunkard of a husband for the sake of her children—and having such nice children. One can learn more from her quiet courage than from many a book.

1920

Good old Gordon came to me today to advise
me that so-and-so might join the church but
that he had been told that I talked considerably
on political issues and he did not like politics in
church. I told my friend that I did not like political lectures in a worship service myself, but
that every religious problem had ethical implications and every ethical problem had some
political and economic aspect. We had quite a
nice chat about it, though my explanation did
not seem altogether satisfactory. Gordon suggested that I seemed unable to get as many
"prominent" people into the church as I ought.
I told him that we had some very nice people
in our church, but that I had no particular desire or ability to cater to "prominent" people,
especially since there are plenty of churches
who seem to serve this class quite well.

This is as close as I have come to having the
freedom of the pulpit challenged, except of
course by the tacit challenge of an occasional
defection from the ranks. The problem of the
freedom of the pulpit is a real one. But I am
convinced that the simplest way to get liberty is

to take it. The liberty to speak on all vital questions of the day without qualifying the message in a half dozen ways adds sufficient interest to the otherwise stodgy sermon to attract two listeners for every one who is lost by having some pet prejudice disarranged. But that generalization is hardly justified by my meager experience.

1920

I had a great discussion in my young men's
class this morning. Gradually I am beginning to
discover that my failure with the class was due
to my talking too much. Now I let them talk and
the thing is becoming interesting. Of course it
isn't so easy to keep the discussion steered on any
track. Sometimes we talk in circles. But the fellows are at least getting at some of the vital
problems of life and I am learning something
from them. Disciplinary problems have disap-
peared. The only one left is the fellow who is
always trying to say something foolish or smart
in the discussion.

1920

I went to the funeral of Mrs. T. at St. Cecilia's church. It must be a grateful task to deal as a priest with the definite symbols which the Catholic church uses and to dispense the absolute certainties with which she assures the faithful. Of course the requiem mass contains nothing that would be of obvious comfort to the sorrowing heart. But the implication of the whole transaction is that the soul is now taken up in another world in which the heartaches of this life are overcome.

I don't think the mass is so satisfying as a well conducted Protestant funeral service in which some cognizance is taken of the peculiar circumstances of a great sorrow and of the unique characteristics of the deceased. But it is certainly immeasurably superior to the average Protestant service with its banalities and sentimentalities. Religion is poetry. The truth in the poetry is vivified by adequate poetic symbols and is therefore more convincing than the poor prose with which the average preacher must attempt to grasp the ineffable.

Yet one must not forget that the truth is not

only vivified but also corrupted by the poetic symbol, for it is only one step from a vivid symbol to the touch of magic. The priest does, after all, deal with magic. When religion renounces magic it finds itself in the poor workaday world trying to discover the glimpses of the eternal in the common scene. That is not an easy task, but it is not an impossible one. Wherefore let us envy the priest, but pity him too, meanwhile. He has been betrayed by his magic. He has gained too easy a victory over life's difficulties and he helps his people to find a premature peace. The rivers of life in Protestant religion are easily lost in the sand, but if they really run they carry more life than holy water.

1921

I spoke to the —— club today and was introduced by the chairman as a pastor who had recently built a new church at "the impressive cost of $170,000." While the figure was not quite correct it gave me somewhat of a start to find how much emphasis was placed upon what was regarded as a great business achievement. Here was a group of business men, and the chairman knew of no way to recommend me to them but by suggesting that I was myself a business man of no mean ability. That would have given the good men of my church council a laugh. Knowing how little I had to do with the raising of the money for the new church and how I have always failed to put on the kind of "pressure" they desired when we were raising money, they would certainly have smiled wryly at this eulogy.

But it is all natural enough. America worships success and so does the world in general. And the only kind of success the average man can understand is obvious success. There must be

"Things done that took the eye, that had the price;

O'er which from level stand,
The low world laid its hand,
Found straightway to its mind, could value in
    a trice."

After all the real work of a minister is not easily gauged and the world may not be entirely wrong in using external progress as an outward sign of an inward grace. Even those who value the real work of the ministry sometimes express their appreciation in rather superficial phrases. I remember when dear old —— celebrated his twenty-fifth anniversary the good toastmaster pathetically described his pastor's successful ministry by explaining that under his leadership the congregation had "doubled its membership, installed a new organ, built a parsonage, decorated the church and wiped out its debt." Not a word about the words of comfort the good pastor had spoken or the inspiration he had given to thirsting souls.

Perhaps it is foolish to be too sensitive about these inevitable secularizations of religious values. Let us be thankful that there is no quarterly meeting in our denomination and no need of giving a district superintendent a bunch of statistics to prove that our ministry is successful.

1921

I visited Mrs. S. today. She is suffering from
cancer and will not live long. Her young grand-
son E. came home from high school just as I was
leaving. He had a question for me. The Jewish
boys at school told him Jesus was a bastard and
Joseph was not his father. He also reported that
they accused him of having two Gods instead of
one. That dissolution of the Trinity into a dualism by high school boys interested me. Even
boys seem to sense that if orthodox trinitarianism
makes for polytheism it really suggests two Gods
rather than three. I chided E. for remembering
so poorly what he had learned in the preparatory
class and for being so irregular in church school
where these problems are discussed. I went over
some of the ideas on the humanity and the
uniqueness of Jesus which we had discussed in
the class.

Meanwhile I wished that I could talk to him
alone without interference from grandma, who
naïvely added her own theological mustard to
the dish. It is no easy task to build up the faith
of one generation and not destroy the supports
of the religion of the other. But fortunately the

old lady didn't get what I was driving at and so didn't interfere very seriously. She was thankful to me for straightening the young man out on his theology and seemed to think that I had settled all his difficulties by my few words. "Ich habe ihm gesagt, wart bis der Pastor kommt. Der wird dir alles erklaeren." It isn't a bad idea to find someone who has such confidence in you.

1922

When I sit in my study and meditate upon men and events I am critical and circumspect. Why is it that when I arise in the pulpit I try to be imaginative and am sometimes possessed by a kind of madness which makes my utterances extravagant and dogmatic? Perhaps this change of technique is due to my desire to move the audience. Audiences are not easily moved from their lethargy by cool and critical analyses. An appeal to the emotions is necessary and emotions are not aroused by a careful analysis of facts but by a presentation of ideal values. I do not mean that I disavow the critical method entirely in the pulpit. Indeed many of my friendly critics think I am too critical to be a good preacher. Nor am I ever very emotional. Nevertheless there is a distinct difference between my temper in the study and my spirit in the pulpit.

Perhaps this is as it should be. Let the study serve to reveal the relativity of all things so that pulpit utterances do not become too extravagant, and let the pulpit save the student from sinking in the sea of relativities. However quali-

fied every truth may be there is nevertheless a
portion in every truth and value which is essentially absolute and which is therefore worth
proclaiming. "All oratory," declares a Greek
scholar, "is based on half truths." That is why
one ought naturally to distrust and to discount
the orator. On the other hand, oratory may be
the result of the kind of poetic gift which sees
a truth dissociated, for a moment at least, from
all relativities of time and circumstance and
lifted into the light of the absolute.

I notice that the tendency of extravagance in
the pulpit and on the platform increases with
the size of the crowd. As my congregation increases in size I become more unguarded in my
statements. Wherefore may the good Lord de-
liver me from ever being a popular preacher.
"Why is it," asked one of my elders the other
day, "that your Sunday evening sermons are
more pessimistic than your morning sermons?"
I think what he really meant is that they were
more critical in analyzing life's problems. I told
him that I tried to give inspiration in the morning and education in the evening.

But the fact is that circumstance probably
affects the quality of the message as much as
purpose. A full church gives me the sense of
fighting with a victorious host in the battles of

the Lord. A half empty church immediately symbolizes the fact that Christianity is very much of a minority movement in a pagan world and that it can be victorious only by snatching victory out of defeat.

1922

Just received a pitiful letter from a young pastor who is losing his church because he has been "too liberal." I suppose there are churches which will crucify a leader who tries to lead them into the modern world of thought and life. Yet here I have been all these years in a conservative communion and have never had a squabble about theology. I suppose that is partly due to the fact that there were so few people here when I came that no one had to listen to me if he didn't like my approach. Those who have come have associated themselves with us because they were in general agreement with "our gospel." They have come, however, from conservative communions and churches. But of course they have been mostly young people.

If preachers get into trouble in pursuance of their task of reinterpreting religious affirmations in the light of modern knowledge I think it must be partly because they beat their drums too loudly when they make their retreats from untenable positions of ancient orthodoxy. The correct strategy is to advance at the center with beating drums and let your retreats at the wings follow as a matter of course and in the interest of the central strategy. You must be honest, of course, but you might just as well straighten and shorten your lines without mock heroics and a fanfare of trumpets.

The beauty of this strategy is that there is enough power at the center for a real advance and enough opposition for a real conflict. If you set the message of a gospel of love against a society enmeshed in hatreds and bigotries and engulfed in greed, you have a real but not necessarily a futile conflict on your hands. There is enough natural grace in the human heart to respond to the challenge of the real message in the gospel—and enough original sin in human nature to create opposition to it. The sorriest preachers are those who preach a conventional morality while they try to be intellectually and theologically radical.

Men will not make great intellectual readjustments for a gospel which does not greatly matter. If there is real adventure at the center of the line the reserves are drawn from the wings almost unconsciously.

1923

Gradually the whole horrible truth about the war is being revealed. Every new book destroys some further illusion. How can we ever again believe anything when we compare the solemn pretensions of statesmen with the cynically conceived secret treaties? Here was simply a tremendous contest for power between two great alliances of states in which the caprice of statesmen combined with basic economic conflicts to dictate the peculiar form of the alliances. Next time the cards will be shuffled in a different way and the "fellowship in arms" will consist of different fellows.

As the truth becomes known there are however some compensations for the disillusionment. If the moral pretensions of the heroes were bogus, the iniquity of the villains was not as malicious as it once appeared. The Kaiser was evidently a boob who was puerile enough to permit the German navalists to force him into policies which he did not understand. Von Tirpitz and his crowd may have been the real villains but they probably did not want the war so much as they wanted to glorify the navy and themselves through it. If Poincaré was the villain, it was the limitations of a narrow and bigoted nationalism rather than the malice of an evil heart which prompted his policies. The poor little Czar was the victim of a neurotic wife, and she in turn the tool of religious fanatics and fear-tormented bureaucrats.

There doesn't seem to be very much malice in the world. There is simply not enough intelligence to conduct the intricate affairs of a complex civilization. All the chief actors in the war appear now in the light of children who played with dangerous toys. If they were criminal it was in the sense that the weal of millions was involved in their dangerous games and they didn't let that fact dissuade them from their play. All human sin seems so much worse in its consequences than in its intentions.

But that is not a fact which justifies moral nihilism. The consequences are obvious and inevitable enough to deter a sensitive soul from the course which leads to destruction. Not merely ignorance but callousness to human welfare is an ingredient in the compound of social and personal evil.

In one sense modern civilization substitutes unconscious sins of more destructive consequences for conscious sins of less destructive consequences. Men try consciously to eliminate

the atrocities of society, but meanwhile they
unheedingly build a civilization which is more
destructive of moral and personal values than
anything intended in a more primitive society.

1923

I met a wonderful parson in the little village of
———. I went there to speak at a high school
commencement. His church seemed to be an
ordinary village church, but he was undeniably
the real leader of the community. Broad sympa-
thies had made it possible for him to transcend
the usual denominational divisions which reduce most ministers to impotence in small communities, at least as far as wider community
leadership is concerned. There were a few
other churches in town, but he had developed
so many types of cooperation between them
that they were almost a unit in their enterprise.

He had built a small church house which was
a hive of activity throughout the week. He conducted his own weekday school of religion,
spending three afternoons at the job. His influence upon the young people was evidently a
fruit of this close contact with them. He was so
happy in his work that he did not look upon
big city churches as the natural goal of his ambition. His wife and he and two little kiddies
live very modestly in a little parsonage, and the
mistress of the manse seems to find time to

mother the neighborhood as well as her children.

Perhaps I am inclined to romanticize about village life. Sometimes it is very petty and mean, I know. But the absence of great class distinctions makes for a higher type of fellowship in church and community than is achieved in the metropolis, and the preacher is not tempted to placate the powerful. The modest stipend which the small church can afford makes for simple living and the absence of social pride. If more young fellows would be willing to go into churches like that and not suffer from inferiority complexes because they had not landed one of the "big pulpits," we might put new power into the church.

Fortunately, this young fellow has an astute intelligence without being an orator. If he were a more gifted speaker he would probably have been "promoted"—and spoiled—long ago. I have often observed that privilege and power tend to corrupt the simple Christian heart. I am now convinced that to these two must be added the kind of obvious success which the world knows how to measure. The simplicity which is preserved because it does not meet the temptation of success is innocence rather than virtue; but if we can't have virtue, innocence is preferable to moral failure.

There are successful men who have maintained a virtuous humility and sincerity in the day of success, but the achievement is very difficult.

1923

In Europe

I have been spending a few days with S——
and P—— in the Ruhr district. Flew back to
London from Cologne by aeroplane. The Ruhr
cities are the closest thing to hell I have ever
seen. I never knew that you could see hatred
with the naked eye, but in the Ruhr one is
under the illusion that this is possible. The
atmosphere is charged with it. The streets are
filled with French soldiers in their grey-blue
uniforms. Schools have been turned into bar-
racks. Germans turn anxious and furtive glances
upon every stranger. French officers race their
automobiles wildly through the streets with
sirens blowing shrilly. If you can gain the confidence of Germans so that they will talk they
will tell you horrible tales of atrocities, deporta-
tions, sex crimes, etc. Imagination fired by fear
and hatred undoubtedly tends to elaborate
upon the sober facts. But the facts are bad
enough.

When we arrived at Cologne after spending
days in the French zone of occupation we felt as
if we had come into a different world. The obvi-

ous reluctance of the British to make common cause with the French in the Ruhr adventure has accentuated the good will between the
British troops and the native population. But
a day in Cologne cannot erase the memory of
Essen and Duesseldorf. It rests upon the mind
like a horrible nightmare. One would like to
send every sentimental spellbinder of war days
into the Ruhr. This, then, is the glorious issue
for which the war was fought! I didn't know
Europe in 1914, but I can't imagine that the
hatred between peoples could have been worse
than it is now.

This is as good a time as any to make up my
mind that I am done with the war business. Of
course, I wasn't really in the last war. Would
that I had been! Every soldier, fighting for his
country in simplicity of heart without asking
many questions, was superior to those of us who
served no better purpose than to increase or perpetuate the moral obfuscation of nations. Of
course, we really couldn't know everything we
know now. But now we know. The times of
man's ignorance God may wink at, but now he
calls us all to repent. I am done with this business. I hope I can make that resolution stick.

Talking about the possibility of the church
renouncing war, as we came over on the boat,
one of the cynics suggested that the present

temper of the church against war was prompted
by nausea rather than idealism. He insisted that
the church would not be able to prove for some
time that it is really sincere in this matter. I suppose he is right; though I do not know that one
ought to be contemptuous of any experience
which leads to the truth. A pain in the stomach
may sometimes serve an ultimate purpose quite
as well as an idea in the head. Yet it is probably
true that nausea finally wears off and the question will then be whether there is a more fundamental force which will maintain a conviction
in defiance of popular hysteria.

For my own part I am not going to let my
decision in regard to war stand alone. I am
going to try to be a disciple of Christ, rather
than a mere Christian, in all human relations
and experiment with the potency of trust and
love much more than I have in the past.

1923

This has been a wonderful Christmas season. The people have been splendid. It is fun to go into the homes and see the laughter and joy of the children. It is rewarding to see how the people respond to our call for Christmas giving among the poor. The church was piled high yesterday with groceries and toys of every description. There is so much that is good in human nature.

Of course the cynics will say that it is easier to be charitable than to be just, and the astute social observers will note that what we give for the needy is but a small fraction of what we spend on ourselves. After all, the spirit of love is still pretty well isolated in the family life. If I had a family maybe that thought would never occur to me. The old Methodist preacher who told me some time ago that I was so cantankerous in my spirit of criticism about modern society because I am not married may be right. If I had about four children to love I might not care so much about insisting that the spirit of love shall dominate all human affairs. And there might be more value in loving the four children than in paying lip service to the spirit of love as I do.

1924

A revival meeting seems never to get under my skin. Perhaps I am too fish-blooded to enjoy them. But I object not so much to the emotionalism as to the lack of intellectual honesty of the average revival preacher. I do not mean to imply that the evangelists are necessarily consciously dishonest. They just don't know enough about life and history to present the problem of the Christian life in its full meaning. They are always assuming that nothing but an emotional commitment to Christ is needed to save the soul from its sin and chaos. They seem never to realize how many of the miseries of mankind are due not to malice but to misdirected zeal and unbalanced virtue. They never help the people who corrupt family love by making the family a selfish unit in society or those who brutalize industry by excessive devotion to the prudential virtues.

Of course that is all inevitable enough. If you don't simplify issues you can't arouse emotional crises. It's the melodrama that captivates the crowd. Sober history is seldom melodramatic. God and the devil may be in conflict on the scene of life and history, but a victory follows every defeat and some kind of defeat every victory. The representatives of God are seldom divine and the minions of Satan are never quite diabolical.

I wonder whether there is any way of being potent oratorically without over-simplifying truth. Or must power always be bought at the expense of truth? Perhaps some simplification of life is justified. Every artist does, after all, obscure some details in order to present others in bolder relief. The religious rhetorician has a right to count himself among, and take his standards from, the artists rather than the scientists. The trouble is that he is usually no better than a cartoonist.

1924

After preaching tonight at a union service in —— the pastor loci took me about to show me his "plant" (industrialism has invaded even ecclesiastical terminology) and with obvious pride told me of all the progress that the church had made since his advent. One of the most disillusioning experiences which I have had with ministers is their invariable tendency to belittle or to be unappreciative of the work of their predecessors. If one were to take the implications of their remarks about their churches without a grain of salt one would imagine that every church was in an obvious state of spiritual and organic decay before the present generation of prophets took hold of the desperate situation. There are, of course, marked exceptions to this rule. But there is too much of this petty jealousy of former laborers in the vineyard of the Lord. Some of the men are probably victims of fawning parishioners and others are just naturally petty.

1924

I am not surprised that most prophets are itin-
erants. Critics of the church think we preachers
are afraid to tell the truth because we are eco-
nomically dependent upon the people of our
church. There is something in that, but it does
not quite get to the root of the matter. I certainly could easily enough get more money
than I am securing now, and yet I catch myself
weighing my words and gauging their possible
effect upon this and that person. I think the real
clue to the tameness of a preacher is the difficulty one finds in telling unpleasant truths to
people whom one has learned to love.

To speak the truth in love is a difficult, and
sometimes an almost impossible, achievement.
If you speak the truth unqualifiedly, that is usually because your ire has been aroused or because you have no personal attachment to the
object of your strictures. Once personal contact
is established you are very prone to temper your
wind to the shorn sheep. It is certainly difficult
to be human and honest at the same time. I'm
not surprised that most budding prophets are
tamed in time to become harmless parish priests.

At that, I do not know what business I have carping at the good people who are doing the world's work and who are inevitably enmeshed to a greater or less degree in the iniquities of society. Conscience, Goethe has observed, belongs to the observer rather than the doer, and it would be well for every preacher to realize that he is morally sensitive partly because he is observing and not acting. What is satisfying about the ministry is to note how far you can go in unfolding the full meaning of the Christian gospel provided you don't present it with the implication that you have attained and are now laying it as an obligation upon others.

If the Christian adventure is made a mutual search for truth in which the preacher is merely a leader among many searchers and is conscious of the same difficulties in his own experience which he notes in others, I do not see why he cannot be a prophet without being forced into itinerancy.

1924

In Europe

We began the day with a visit to the York minster and ended it with a dinner at the Rountree
cocoa works. Some of the men thought there
was more spirituality in the discussion of the
ethical problems of modern industry in which
we engaged at Rountree's than in the communion service we heard so atrociously read in
the minster. Of course the dinner discussion was
richer in ethical content, but there are nevertheless religious values in the cathedral which one
cannot find in a discussion of ethical problems
however vital.

Religion is a reaction to life's mysteries and
a reverence before the infinitudes of the universe. Without ethical experience the infinite
is never defined in ethical terms, but the soul
which is reverent and morally vital at the same
time learns how to apprehend the infinite in
terms of holiness and worships a God who tran-
scends both our knowledge and our conscience.
The cathedral with its dim religious light, its
vaulted ceiling, its altar screen, and its hushed

whispers is symbolic of the element of mystery in religion.

Without an adequate sermon no clue is given to the moral purpose at the heart of the mystery, and reverence remains without ethical content. But a religion which never goes beyond a sense of awe is no more complete (though perhaps less serviceable) than one which has reduced life's ultimate and ineffable truth to a pat little formula which a proud little man expounds before a comfortable and complacent congregation. I am sorry that there is no more ethically vital preaching in the cathedral, though that wretched communion service this morning, which could help no one if he did not believe in magic, is hardly typical of everything which happens in a cathedral. But I am equally sorry that the sense of awe and reverence has departed from so many of our churches.

The very appearance of many of our churches betrays the loss of one necessary element in religion. Everything suggests the secular rather than the religious, from the red hat of the rather too sensuously pretty soprano soloist and the frock coat of the rather too self-conscious parson to the comfortable pew cushions and the splendiferous pew holders. The morning sun shines brightly into the "auditorium" and the

sun of worldly wisdom illumines the discourse
of the preacher.

Of course I know that the devotional attitude
frequently destroys clear thinking, and we need
clear thinking for ethical living in a complex
civilization. But it ought not be impossible to
preserve the poetic with the scientific attitude,
the mystical with the analytical, to have both
worship and instruction. I think that is what
Heywood Broun was driving at some time ago
when he expressed a preference for an "Episcopal church with an heretical sermon." Unfortunately the heretical, i.e., the morally vital and
contemporaneous religious instruction, does not
seem to flourish in the liturgical church.

But there are men here in England who
preach prophetic sermons in cathedrals. There
might be more. In America they are certainly
not numerous. But that is no reason why we
should dismiss religious awe and reverence as
morally dangerous. After all, the prophetic
preaching which we hear in our "church audi-
toriums" is not so vigorous as to give us any
certainty that a secularized church is superior
in its moral potency.

1924

While visiting at the home of Mr. and Mrs. —— today little Ralph felt it incumbent upon himself to entertain me by putting the family dog through his tricks. I have already forgotten the breed of the dog, but his shaggy locks covered his eyes so completely that he seemed to be without eyesight. Ralph told me with great eagerness that the dog would go blind if his locks were cut to improve his eyesight. Thus nature adjusts herself to her own inadequacies, and women of the future may run the peril of deafness if they uncover their ears.

Ralph's dog gave me the clue to much of our irreligion. The eyes of so many people have been covered by superstitions and illusions that they are not strong enough to preserve their sight in the daylight of knowledge. Freed from their superstitions, they are blinded in the very moment that they are given an unhindered view. They could see beauty while they lived in twilight, but a brilliant light obscures life's beauty and meaning.

Of course the eye may ultimately adjust itself to the brilliance of the light, and as men grow accustomed to the concrete and specific objects which distract them on first sight, they will learn again to view the whole scene and to regard all things in their relationships.

It is in relationships and in totalities that life's meaning is revealed.

1924

Since spending the summer in Europe I have
been devoting the entire fall to a development
of our worship service. The various types of
ritualistic services in non-conformist churches I
heard over there appealed to me so much that
I decided to imitate them. Of course the Angli-
can services have their own appeal, but the
technique which makes them possible is beyond
us. For some years I have been having a few
prayer responses, but now I am developing a
program with litanies, confessions, acts of praise
and every other bit of liturgical beauty and
meaning by which the service can be enriched.

It's a shame we have permitted our services
to become so barren. My only regret is that I
did not wake up in time to build our church
properly for liturgical purposes. There could be
much pleasure in conducting a richly elaborated
liturgical service without the restraint of the
rubrics to which the Anglicans must submit. I
do not know whether the people like the added
beauty in the service as much as I do, but many
have expressed appreciation. It seems to me to
make a great deal of difference in the spiritual

value of a service to have some unison prayer
with an authentic religious emotion expressed
in a well turned phrase, to have choir responses
for the prayers and moments of silence for quiet
prayer.

The idea that a formless service is more spon-
taneous and therefore more religious than a
formal one is disproved in my own experience.
Only a very few men have ever really put me in
a mood of prayer by their "pastoral prayers." On
the other hand, a really beautiful worship service actually gives me a mystic sense of the divine.

1924

Arrived in —— today and spoke this noon to a group of liberal people. The meeting was arranged by the secretary of the Y.W.C.A. I poked fun at them a little for enjoying their theological liberalism so much in this part of the country, while they were afraid of even the mildest economic and political heresy. Of course that didn't quite apply to the people at the table, but it does apply to this whole section. There is no one quite so ridiculous as a preacher who prides himself upon his theological radicalism in a city where the theological battle was won a generation ago, while he meanwhile speaks his convictions on matters of economics only in anxious whispers.

I was asked to visit —— (leading preacher) and see whether I could not interest him in our organization. He was an interesting study. He told me of his important connections in the city, of his tremendous church program, of the way he had increased the budget of his church, of his building plans, of the necessity "of fighting on one front at a time," of his theological battles; and he ended by declining to join the liberal group which sought his aid.

He thought it would not be advisable, considering his heavy responsibilities, to imperil the many great "causes" to which he was devoting his life by identifying himself with a radical movement. I didn't mind his cowardice so much, though he tried to hide it, as his vanity, which he took no pains to hide. I could just see him cavorting weekly before his crowd of doting admirers.

Obviously one of his chief difficulties is that he is good looking. A minister has enough temptations to vanity without bearing the moral hazard of a handsome face. If this young fellow had only been half as homely as old Dr. Gordon he might have a chance of acquiring a portion of his grace. But I don't want to drive that generalization too far. I know one or two saintly preachers who could pose for a collar ad.

1924

Had a letter today informing me that the First
—— church in —— has called a new pastor.
After trying futilely to find the right man, who
was to have as much scholarship as his prede-
cessor and more "punch," they decided to raise
the salary to $15,000. I don't know whether that
was the factor which finally solved their problem, but at any rate they have the man they
want. I suppose it is not easy to get a combina-
tion of Aristotle and Demosthenes, and on the
current market, that ought to be worth $15,000.
Nevertheless there must be some limit to this
matter of oversized salaries.

There ought to be some questioning, too,
about the growing tendency of churches to
build their congregations around pulpit eloquence. What kind of fundamental ethical question can a man be eloquent about when he
draws that much cash, particularly since a Croe-
sus or two usually has to supply an undue proportion of it? I don't know anything about the
prophet of the Lord who accepted this call, but
I venture to prophesy that no sinner in that

pagan city will quake in his boots in anticipation of his coming.

The idea of a professional good man is difficult enough for all of us who are professionally engaged as teachers of the moral ideal. Of course, "a man must live," and it is promised that if we seek first the kingdom and its righteousness "all these things shall be added unto us." But I doubt whether Jesus had a $15,000 salary in mind. If the things that are added become too numerous they distract your attention terribly. To try to keep your eye on the main purpose may only result in making you squint-eyed. I hope the new prophet won't begin his pastorate with a sermon on the text, "I count all things but loss."

1924

I was a little ashamed of what I wrote recently about ministers' salaries, but today I was strangely justified in my criticism. Walking into a store to buy a hat I met an old friend who told me about his new preacher. His church had tried for a long while to secure the right man, and then by dint of a special campaign they raised the salary from $6,000 to $10,000. That is obviously more than most of the people in the congregation make. He said to me with considerable pride, "You ought to hear our new preacher. My, but he is a great talker!" Then he came close and whispered to me out of hearing of the other customers: "He ought to be. We are paying him ten thousand dollars." The cynicism was quite unconscious.

1924

I begin to realize how little religious faith depends upon dialectical support. When called upon to bury some one whose life revealed spiritual charm and moral force I can preach the hope of immortality with conviction and power. But funerals of religious and moral nondescripts leave me enervated. I think I could bury a brazen sinner with more satisfaction. There is always a note of real tragedy in the life of an obvious reprobate that gives point to a sermon. But these Tomlinsons are a trial.

Of course, there is a good deal of pride in such an attitude, and it is partly due to ignorance. As soon as I know the person whose death is mourned I can enter into the occasion sympathetically. There is hardly a soul so poor and flaccid but does not reveal some glimpse of the eternal in its life. If I happen to lack contact with the deceased I might well remind myself that his death is sincerely mourned by those who are near. It is after all a glorious tribute to the qualities of human nature that those who know us best love us most. Perhaps their love is occasionally no more than a natural attachment which men conceive for familiar objects.

Funerals are a terrible trial to me, but I must admit that the stolid courage and quiet grief of most mourners is a real source of inspiration. Only occasionally does one meet with hysterical grief and theatrical and insincere sorrow. How desperately people brush up their little faith in times of sorrow! It is quite easy to see that religious faith prospers because of, and not in spite of, the tribulations of this world. It is because this mortal life is felt as an irrelevancy to the main purpose in life that men achieve the courage to hope for immortality.

1924

We had a union Thanksgiving service today. It would have been a nice service but for the fact that the leader could not get over the fact that four denominations had been able to achieve unity to undertake such a service. This was supposed to be a great advance. As a matter of fact the people in the church were long since united in dozens of community enterprises. The men, whatever church they belonged to, attended the same Rotary and Kiwanis clubs and the women were members of the same literary and review clubs.

The church has lost the chance of becoming the unifying element in our American society. It is not anticipating any facts. It is merely catching up very slowly to the new social facts created by economic and other forces. The American melting pot is doing its work. The churches merely represent various European cultures, lost in the amalgam of American life and maintaining a separate existence only in religion.

What we accomplish in the way of church unity ought to be accepted with humility and not hailed with pride. We are not creating. We are merely catching up with creation.

1924

Going to St. Louis today a portly and garrulous gentleman sat back of me and became very much interested in two nuns who were reading their prayerbooks. The man, who seemed the perfect type of successful drummer, felt very superior to the nuns. How can anyone "fall for that stuff" in this day and age, he wanted to know in a loud whisper. "They remind me of ghosts," he said.

I had to admit that there was something almost unearthly about these black figures with their white-rimmed hoods. But their faces were kindly and human, and the face of the drummer was sensuous and florid. Perhaps the difference between him and the nuns illustrates the quality of our "modernity," though I don't want to maintain that he is the perfect type of a modern man. But we do have a great many moderns who are emancipated from every kind of religious discipline without achieving any new loyalty which might qualify the brutal factors in human life.

It is better that life incarnate some ideal value, even if mixed with illusion (though anything which has the spirit of love in it is not wholly illusion) than that it should express nothing but the will to live. My drummer thinks of himself as a modern in comparison with those nuns. I looked at him squatting there and glanced again at the homely but beautiful faces of the nuns and said to myself: What is modern and what is ancient? Were there not toads before there were ghosts and fairies?

1924

Bishop Williams is dead. I sit and stare at the floor while I say that to myself and try to believe it. How strangely a vital personality defies the facts of death. Nowhere have I seen a personality more luminous with the Christ spirit than in this bishop who was also a prophet. Here was a man who knew how to interpret the Christian religion so that it meant something in terms of an industrial civilization. His fearless protagonism of the cause of democracy in industry won him the respect and love of the workers of the city as no other churchman possessed it.

Yet I am afraid that it must be admitted that he didn't change the prevailing attitude of Detroit industry by a hair's breadth. He even had to offer his resignation in the face of increasing hostility to his social views. That letter of resignation was incidentally a gem of humble self-analysis and courageous insistence on the truth of his doctrine.

He did not change Detroit industry but he left many of us holding our heads more upright because of his intelligent and courageous analysis of contemporary civilization from the perspective of a Christian conscience. If a bishop with all his prestige could make no bigger dent upon the prevailing mood of the city, what chance is there for the rest of us? Perhaps the best that any of us can do is to say:

> *Charge once more then and be dumb,*
> *Let the victors when they come,*
> *When the forts of folly fall,*
> *Find thy body by the wall.*

Rejoice, said Jesus, not that the devils are subject unto you but that your names are written in heaven. One ought to strive for the reformation of society rather than one's own perfection. But society resists every effort to bring its processes under ethical restraint so stubbornly that one must finally be satisfied with preserving one's moral integrity in a necessary and yet futile struggle. Of course the struggle is never as futile as it seems from an immediate perspective. The bishop did not change Detroit industry, but if the church ever becomes a real agency of the kingdom of God in an industrial civilization, his voice, though he is dead, will be in its counsels.

1925

When I sit through a church conference I begin
to see a little more clearly why religion is on
the whole so impotent ethically, why the
achievements of the church are so meager com-
pared to its moral pretensions. Sermon after
sermon, speech after speech is based upon the
assumption that the people of the church are
committed to the ethical ideals of Jesus and that
they are the sole or at least chief agents of
redemptive energy in society.

It is very difficult to persuade people who are
committed to a general ideal to consider the
meaning of that ideal in specific situations. It is
even more difficult to prompt them to consider
specific ends of social and individual conduct
and to evaluate them in the light of experience.

The church conference begins and ends by
attempting to arouse an emotion of the ideal,
usually in terms of personal loyalty to the person of Jesus, but very little is done to attach the
emotion to specific tasks and projects. Is the
industrial life of our day unethical? Are nations
imperialistic? Is the family disintegrating? Are
young people losing their sense of values? If so,

we are told over and over again that nothing
will help but "a new baptism of the spirit," a
"new revival of religion," a "great awakening
of the religious consciousness."

But why not be specific? Why doesn't the
church offer specific suggestions for the application of a Christian ethic to the difficulties of our
day? If that suggestion is made, the answer is
that such a policy would breed contention. It
certainly would. No moral project can be presented and no adventure made without resistance from the traditionalist and debate among
experimentalists. But besides being more effective, such a course would be more interesting
than this constant bathing in sentimentalities.
If the church could only achieve schisms on
ethical issues! They would represent life and
reality. Its present schisms are not immoral as
such. They are immoral only in the sense that
they perpetuate issues which have no relevancy
in our day.

1925

The reactions of a group of ministers to an address on the relation of religion to modern life are always interesting. Invariably there is one group of men who are pathetically eager to "do something about it," to save civilization from its perils. I think the church will compare favorably with the university in the number of men who are not blinded to the defects of modern life and who are not enervated by a sense of futility. The university has plenty of men whose eyes are open, but they despair much more easily of finding a way out than the preachers. The ministers have not lost some of that saving grace, "the foolishness of faith."

Of course there is always a group of those who sit sullenly while you harangue them. I had my eye fixed on one portly and prosperous priest today who was obviously out of accord with what I was saying. Of course I have no right to judge him because he did not agree with me. But he seemed to me to be one of those satisfied and complacent chaplains who has fed so long at the flesh-pots of Egypt that he resents anything which disturbs his ease. A man like that reminds me of the eunuchs of old who were robbed of their virility that they might adorn without endangering their masters' luxurious establishments.

The old gentleman was there too who wanted to know whether I believed in the deity of Jesus. He is in every town. He seemed to be a nice sort, but he wanted to know how I could speak for an hour on the Christian church without once mentioning the atonement. Nothing, said he, but the blood of Jesus would save America from its perils. He made quite an impassioned speech. At first I was going to answer him but it seemed too useless. I finally told him I believed in blood atonement too, but since I hadn't shed any of the blood of sacrifice which it demanded I felt unworthy to enlarge upon the idea.

1925

We went through one of the big automobile factories today. So artificial is life that these factories are like a strange world to me though I have lived close to them for many years. The foundry interested me particularly. The heat was terrific. The men seemed weary. Here manual labor is a drudgery and toil is slavery. The men cannot possibly find any satisfaction in their work. They simply work to make a living. Their sweat and their dull pain are part of the price paid for the fine cars we all run. And most of us run the cars without knowing what price is being paid for them.

Looking at these men the words of Markham's "The Man with the Hoe" came to me. A man with a hoe is a happy creature beside these suffering souls.

"The emptiness of ages in his face"

.   .   .   .

"Who made him dead to rapture and despair,
A thing that grieves not and that never hopes,
Stolid and stunned, a brother to the ox?"

We are all responsible. We all want the things which the factory produces and none of us is sensitive enough to care how much in human values the efficiency of the modern factory costs. Beside the brutal facts of modern industrial life, how futile are all our homiletical spoutings! The church is undoubtedly cultivating graces and preserving spiritual amenities in the more protected areas of society. But it isn't changing the essential facts of modern industrial civilization by a hair's breadth. It isn't even thinking about them.

The morality of the church is anachronistic. Will it ever develop a moral insight and courage sufficient to cope with the real problems of modern society? If it does it will require generations of effort and not a few martyrdoms. We ministers maintain our pride and self-respect and our sense of importance only through a vast and inclusive ignorance. If we knew the world in which we live a little better we would perish in shame or be overcome by a sense of futility.

1925

The new parish organization seems to be working splendidly. The congregation is divided into
nine sections, each with a man and woman as
parish leaders. Each section meets twice a year
in cottage meetings, and meanwhile the leaders
and their assistants visit the various families,
particularly the new members and those who
are sick. Some splendid new leaders have already been developed by this plan. Since I must
be absent from the city so much, the plan is all
the more valuable.

Last Sunday we discussed in the class
whether a church ought to develop fellowship
for its own sake or whether fellowship ought to
be the inevitable by-product of unifying convictions. I suppose a small church in a hostile
environment would not have to worry about
fellowship. If people fight shoulder to shoulder
they will be brothers. But even the most heroic
church is not so definitely in conflict with the
society in which it lives that you can really
count on that kind of fellowship. A local congregation is, after all, a social organism in which
heroic idealism is expressed in an occasional ad-

venture, if at all, rather than in a constant tension between its principles and the moral mediocrities of the world.

Meanwhile, it seems to me to be worth while to cultivate the graces of neighborliness merely for their own sake. This is particularly true in the large city where life is so impersonal and where the church has a fine opportunity to personalize it a little. What surprises me is the readiness with which people give themselves to various forms of mutual aid once they are prompted to engage in them.

Most people lack imagination much more than they lack good will. If someone points out what can be done and what ought to be done there is usually someone to do it.

1925

On a Western Trip

Out here on the Pacific coast, particularly in Los Angeles, one is forcibly impressed with the influence of environment upon religion. Every kind of cult seems to flourish in Los Angeles, and most of them are pantheistic. Every sorry oriental religious nostrum is borrowed in the vain effort to give meaning to pointless lives and to impart a thrill to vacuous existences. The pantheism is partly due, no doubt, to the salubrious nature of the southern California climate. Wherever nature is unusually benignant, men tend to identify God and the natural world and to lose all moral vigor in the process.

But that is hardly the whole explanation. There are too many retired people in Los Angeles. They left the communities where their personalities had some social significance in order to vegetate on these pleasant shores. In this sorry and monotonous existence they try to save their self-respect by grasping for some religious faith which will not disturb their ease by any too rigorous ethical demands. Of course Aimee Semple McPherson is more successful than the pantheistic cults. She fights the devil and gives the people a good show. She storms against the vices which flourish in this paradise without touching their roots. Furthermore she has the art of casting the glow of religious imagination over sensuality without changing its essential nature. In that art she seems to be typical rather than unique for this whole civilization. If she is unique it is only in her success.

They are always telling me that Detroit is the most typically American of our cities. Perhaps Detroit is typical of the America which works feverishly to get what it wants, while Los Angeles is typical of the America which has secured what it wants. On the whole I prefer the former to the latter. An honest enthusiasm even for inadequate ends is better than a vacuous existence from which even the charm of an imperfect ambition has departed. Of course the paganism of power is more dangerous than the paganism of pleasure, but from the perspective of a mere observer it is more interesting. Who would not prefer Napoleon to his imbecile brothers who merely luxuriated in the prosperity created by his ambition?

Only in the case of complete innocency, as that of a child's, is life more beautiful in repose than in activity. Character is created by a balance of tensions, and is more lovely even when the balance is imperfect than in a state of complete relaxation.

Of course Los Angeles has more culture than our midwestern cities. Culture flourishes in leisure and sometimes redeems it. But it will be a long time before this kind of leisure will produce more than dilettantism.

1925

We had a communion service tonight (Good Friday) and I preached on the text "We preach Christ crucified, to the Jews a stumbling block and to the Gentiles foolishness, but to them that are called the power of God and the wisdom of God." I don't think I ever felt greater joy in preaching a sermon. How experience and life change our perspectives! It was only a few years ago that I did not know what to make of the cross; at least I made no more of it than to recognize it as a historic fact which proved the necessity of paying a high price for our ideals. Now I see it as a symbol of ultimate reality.

It seems pathetic to me that liberalism has too little appreciation of the tragedy of life to understand the cross and orthodoxy insists too much upon the absolute uniqueness of the sacrifice of Christ to make the preaching of the cross effective. How can anything be uniquely potent if it is absolutely unique? It is because the cross of Christ symbolizes something in the very heart of reality, something in universal experience that it has its central place in history. Life is tragic and the most perfect type of moral beauty inevitably has at least a touch of the tragic in it. Why? That is not so easy to explain. But love pays such a high price for its objectives and sets its objectives so high that they can never be attained. There is therefore always a foolish and a futile aspect to love's quest which give it the note of tragedy.

What makes this tragedy redemptive is that the foolishness of love is revealed as wisdom in the end and its futility becomes the occasion for new moral striving. About heroes, saints, and saviors it must always remain true "that they, without us should not be made perfect."

1925

I wonder if the strong sense of frustration which comes over me so frequently on Sunday evening and to which many other parsons have confessed, is merely due to physical lassitude or whether it arises from the fact that every preacher is trying to do a bigger thing than he is equal to—and fails. I have an uneasy feeling that it may be native honesty of the soul asserting itself. Aren't we preachers talking altogether too much about what can be proved and justified only in experience?

1925

Mr. —— spoke at a luncheon meeting today.
He made everyone writhe as he pictured the injustices and immoralities of our present industrial system. The tremendous effect of his
powerful address was partially offset by the
bitterness with which he spoke and by the ill-
concealed assumption that his hearers would
not care enough about what he said to change
their attitudes. I suppose it is difficult to escape
bitterness when you have the eyes to see and
the heart to feel what others are too blind and
too callous to notice. The mordant note in the
discourse of the prophet may not only be inevitable but pedagogically effective.

Perhaps there is no other way to arouse a people who are so oblivious to the real issues of
modern civilization. Yet I am compelled to
doubt the pedagogical benefits of this approach.
While I use it myself, sometimes I don't like to
have it used on me. It freezes my soul. And
there is usually some injustice, some insupporta-
ble generalization, involved in this method
which obsesses my mind and makes it difficult

for me to see the general truth with which the speaker wants to impress me.

If I had to choose between this bitterness and the blandness of many pulpiteers I would, of course, choose the former. Better a warrior's grimness than the childish sentimentalities of people who are too ignorant or too selfish to bear the burdens of the world. There are too many men in the pulpit who look and act for all the world like cute little altar boys who have no idea that the mass in which they are participating is a dramatization of tragedy.

Yet there seems to be no reason why a warrior ought not to maintain his effectiveness and yet overcome his bitterness, particularly if he is a warrior who is fighting "not against flesh and blood but against spiritual wickedness in high places." The one certain cure for a bitter spirit seems to me a realization that the critic is himself involved in the sins which he castigates. Man is imperialistic and even parasitic in his nature. He lives his life at the expense of other lives. By both outer compulsion and inner restraint, his expansive desires are brought under sufficient discipline to make social life possible.

But there is no social life, not even in the family, which does not illustrate this native imperialism in life. Look at all these professional people, preachers, professors and doctors! Even

in the moment in which they declare their superiority over the commercial world, where life
is more frankly selfish and more obviously brutal, they illustrate the common human frailty
by some petty jockeying for position, or some
jealous depreciation of the success of others,
or some childish ego-assertion.

The pessimist might draw the conclusion
from this fact that we can make progress only
by a reorganization of society and never by a
reformation of human nature. But that conclusion does not seem to me to follow from the
facts. We do need a constant reorganization
of social processes and systems, so that society
will not aggravate but mitigate the native imperialistic impulses of man. The greed of modern civilization is partly an expression of a
universal human tendency and partly a vice
peculiar to a civilization with our kind of productive process.

But meanwhile we can not afford to leave the
capacities of man out of the picture. There
seems to me no reason why we can not cure
people of greed by making them conscious of
both the nature and the consequences of their
expansive tendencies. Only we ought to realize,
while we are doing it, that our own life reveals
some refined form of the sin which we abhor.
That will make it possible to undertake the task

of world regeneration with a spirit of patience and humility.

The modern pulpit does not face this problem because it is not really preaching repentance. Its estimate of human nature is too romantic to give people any appreciation of the brutalities of life which are frequently most real where they are most covert—in the lives of the respectable classes. But whenever a prophet is born, either inside or outside of the church, he does face the problem of preaching repentance without bitterness and of criticizing without spiritual pride.

It is a real problem. Mr. —— is effective, after a fashion, because he is an itinerant. We only have to hear him once in so many years. But think of sitting Sunday after Sunday under some professional holy man who is constantly asserting his egotism by criticizing yours. I would rebel if I were a layman. A spiritual leader who has too many illusions is useless. One who has lost his illusions about mankind and retains his illusions about himself is insufferable. Let the process of disillusionment continue until the self is included. At that point, of course, only religion can save from the enervation of despair. But it is at that point that true religion is born.

1926

Preachers who are in danger of degenerating into common scolds might learn a great deal from H——'s preaching style. I am not thinking now of the wealth of scholarship which enriches his utterances but of his technique in uniting religious emotion with aspiration rather than with duty. If he wants to convict Detroit of her sins he preaches a sermon on "the City of God," and lets all the limitations of this get-rich-quick metropolis emerge by implication. If he wants to flay the denominationalism of the churches he speaks on some topic which gives him the chance to delineate the ideal and inclusive church.

On the whole, people do not achieve great moral heights out of a sense of duty. You may be able to compel them to maintain certain minimum standards by stressing duty, but the highest moral and spiritual achievements depend not upon a push but upon a pull. People must be charmed into righteousness. The language of aspiration rather than that of criticism and command is the proper pulpit language. Of course it has its limitations. In every congregation there are a few perverse sinners who can go into emotional ecstasies about the "City of God" and yet not see how they are helping to make their city a hell-hole.

It is not a good thing to convict sin only by implication. Sometimes the cruel word of censure must be uttered. "Woe unto you Scribes and Pharisees, hypocrites" was spoken by one who incarnated tenderness. The language of aspiration is always in danger of becoming soft; but it is possible to avoid that pitfall and yet not sink into a habit of cheap scolding. I like the way H—— does it.

1926

Cynics sometimes insinuate that you can love people only if you don't know them too well; that a too intimate contact with the foibles and idiosyncrasies of men will tempt one to be a misanthrope. I have not found it so. I save myself from cynicism by knowing individuals, and knowing them intimately. If I viewed humanity only from some distant and high perspective I could not save myself from misanthropy. I think the reason is simply that people are not as decent in their larger relationship as in their more intimate contacts.

Look at the industrial enterprise anywhere and you find criminal indifference on the part of the strong to the fate of the weak. The lust for power and the greed for gain are the dominant note in business. An industrial overlord will not share his power with his workers until he is forced to do so by tremendous pressure. The middle classes, with the exception of a small minority of intelligentsia, do not aid the worker in exerting this pressure. He must fight alone.

The middle classes are in fact quite incapable of any high degree of social imagination. Their experience is too limited to give them a clear picture of the real issues in modern industrial life. Nonunion mines may organize in West Virginia and reduce miners to a starvation wage without challenging the conscience of a great middle class nation. If the children of strikers are starving it is more difficult to find support for them than to win contributors for the missions of the church. America may arouse the resentment of the world by its greed and all the good people of the American prairie will feel nothing but injured innocence from these European and Asiatic reactions to our greed.

Men are clearly not very lovely in the mass. One can maintain confidence in them only by viewing them at close range. Then one may see the moral nobility of unselfish parenthood, the pathetic eagerness of father and mother to give their children more of life than they enjoyed; the faithfulness of wives to their erring husbands; the grateful respect of mature children for their old parents; the effort of this and that courageous soul to maintain personal integrity in a world which continually tempts to dishonesty, and the noble aspirations of hearts that must seem quite unheroic to the unheeding world.

The same middle classes which seem so blind to the larger moral problems of society have, after all, the most wholesome family life of any group in society.

1926

Here is a preacher whom I have suspected of
cowardice for years because he never deviated
by a hair's breadth from the economic prejudices of his wealthy congregation. I thought he
knew better but was simply afraid to speak out
and seek to qualify the arch-conservatism of his
complacent crowd with a little Christian idealism. But I was mistaken. I have just heard that
he recently included in his sermon a tirade
against women who smoke cigarettes and lost
almost a hundred of his fashionable parishioners. He is evidently not lacking courage in matters upon which he has deep convictions.
Nobody, for that matter, lacks courage when
convictions are strong. Courage is simply the
rigorous devotion to one set of values against
other values and interests.

Protestantism's present impotence in qualifying the economic and social life of the nation is
due not so much to the pusillanimity of the
clerical leaders as to its individualistic traditions. The church honestly regards it of greater
moment to prevent women from smoking cigarettes than to establish more Christian standards
in industrial enterprise. A minister who tries to

prevent fashionable women from smoking cigarettes is simply trying to enforce a code of personal habit established in the middle classes of
the nineteenth century upon the plutocratic
classes of the twentieth century. The effort is
not only vain but has little to do with essential
Christianity.

I would not deny that some real values may
be at stake in such questions of personal habits.
But they affect the dominant motives which determine the spirituality or sensuality of character
but slightly. The church does not seem to realize
how unethical a conventionally respectable life
may be.

1926

Some of these young business men in the congregation would compare favorably with any
leaders who grace the pulpits of our churches.
Their family relations seem to be almost ideal.
They are trying honestly to live a Christian life
in their business relations. Lack of power sometimes means that they cannot go as far in experimenting with Christian values as they would
like. But they are not complacent. They are
eager to learn, and are fair and careful in their
judgments. Their virtues are acquired with less
self-conscious effort than those of more studious
people. They think and plan, but they do not
stop the adventure of life to meditate upon its
difficulties and inadequacies.

Extrovert people are on the whole happier
and more wholesome than the introverts. If they
do not act too unreflectively, they are able to
define their goals fairly accurately and they certainly pursue them with more robust energy
than do the moody intellectuals.

It is surprising, too, how considerate and generous they are in their relations with one another
and with me. They take my impetuosities for

granted and exhibit little pettiness in their deal-
ings with one another. The women do not get
along quite so well together. They are too new
at playing the game of life with others. But I
will not belabor that point. I may be exhibiting
bachelor prejudices in making it. At any rate I
am willing to compare this group of young men
who bear the burdens of our church with any
faculty group in the country. They can teach
you nothing about philosophy, but they do teach
you much about life and they reënforce your
confidence in human nature.

1926

After Attending a Jewish-Christian Conference

Fellowship with peoples of other religious groups
always results in the grateful experience of dis-
covering unsuspected treasuries of common sentiment and conviction. More contact between
enlightened Jews and Christians would change
the emphasis in many a Christian homily. This
conference was rewarding in many ways. But at
one point I fail absolutely to understand my
Jewish friends. All of them, high and low, intelligent and those who are less so, insist that the
story of the crucifixion is the real root of all or
of most anti-Semitism, and they seem to have
some vain hope that broadminded Christians
will be able and willing to erase the story of
the cross from the gospel record. The least they
expect is that the odium of the cross be placed
upon the Romans rather than the Jews.

I can see that there would be some advantage
in ascribing a historic sin to a people who live
only in history and who can therefore not be
victimized by belated vindictive prejudices. But
would that be history? The record is pretty

plain and the fact that the Jewish elders rather than Roman soldiers were the real crucifiers is supported not only by evidence but by logic. The prophets of religion are always martyred by the religious rather than by the irreligious. The Romans, being irreligious, were not sufficiently fanatical to initiate the crucifixion.

It must be admitted that the phraseology of the Fourth Gospel may easily incite the prejudices of the ignorant. But the enlightened will find a better method to allay any anti-Semitic feeling which may result from the record than to ascribe the crucifixion to the Romans. They need only ascribe it to the general limitations of human nature and society. Jews are not the only people who martyr and who have martyred their prophets. The history of every nation and every people makes the crucifixion a perennial and a universal historical fact.

That is the very reason why Christians can no more afford to eliminate the cross than they can ascribe it to the fortunately extinct Romans. Anyone who incarnates the strategy of love as Jesus did meets the resistance and incites the passions of human society. The respectabilities of any human society are based upon moral compromises and every community is as anxious to defend these compromises against the prophet who presents some higher moral logic as against the criminal who imperils the structure from below.

The cross is central in the Christian religion, moreover, because it symbolizes a cosmic as well as an historic truth. Love conquers the world, but its victory is not an easy one. The price of all creativity and redemption is pain. Most modern religionists who understand the God of creation and not the God of redemption fail in understanding the latter precisely because they do not see how closely related creation and redemption are. Which simply means that they don't understand that creation is a painful process in which the old does not give way to the new without trying to overcome it.

The cross of Jesus is truly the most adequate symbol of both the strategy and the destiny of love not only in history but in the universe. We may grant our Jewish brethren that it is not the only possible symbol of eternal verities, but it is a true one, and it cannot therefore be sacrificed.

Incidentally, I believe that Jewish people have a tendency to overestimate the religious bases of anti-Semitism. Racial rather than religious prejudice is the dominant factor in this social disease. All ignorant people hate or fear those who deviate from their type. Religious divergences may be as important as cultural and physical differences, but they are not dominant.

The Jews could accept our religion and if they maintained their racial integrity they would still suffer from various types of social ostracism. After all the Negroes are Christian, but that hasn't helped them much. Some Jews dislike this comparison very much. They do not like to be put upon the same basis with the Negroes. But that reveals unrealistic social analysis. The majority group is intolerant of minorities whether their culture is inferior, superior or equal.

1926

One is hardly tempted to lose confidence in the future after listening to a group of young people discussing the important problems of life. Of course the number who approach the future reflectively and with real appreciation for the issues involved in the readjustment of traditions to new situations is not large. There are not many such groups and even in these the number who really take part in the discussion is small.

Nevertheless their wholesomeness is impressive. I can't always withhold a sense of pity for them. With traditions crumbling and accepted standards inundated by a sea of moral relativity, they have a desperate task on their hands to construct new standards adequate for their happiness. There is always the temptation to be too rebellious or too traditional, to be scornful of the old standard even when it preserves obvious virtues, or to flee to it for fear of being lost in the confusion of new standards. Yet the best way of avoiding these dangers is to subject them to the scrutiny of a thoughtful group which knows how to discern the limitations of any position, old or new.

On the whole the discussions of our young people at the church seem to be more wholesome than those in which I participate in the colleges. Most of these young folks have assumed responsibilities and are therefore not as inclined to be morbidly critical and skeptical as the college group. The cases cited from their own experience help to give vitality to their discussion, and they are not enervated by that extreme sophistication which imperils the college youth and tempts him to end every discussion and discount every discovery with the reflection, "This also is vanity."

I really wonder how we are going to build a civilization sufficiently intelligent to overcome dangerous prejudices and to emancipate itself from the inadequacies of conventional morality without creating the kind of sophistication which destroys all values by its skepticism and dampens every enthusiasm by its cynicism. In America that possibility is particularly dangerous because our intellectualism is of the sophomoric type. There is no generation, or only one generation, between the pioneers who conquered the prairies and these youngsters who are trying to absorb the whole of modern culture in four years. The traditions against which they react are less adequate, less modified by experience and culture, than those which inform the peoples of Europe.

And the teachers who guide them into the world of new knowledge are frequently themselves so recently emancipated that they try to obscure their cultural, religious and moral heritages by extreme iconoclasm. It is difficult to be patient with one of these smart aleck Ph.D.'s on a western campus who imagines that he can impress the world with his learning by being scornful of everything that was thought or done before this century.

1926

A letter from Hyde brings the sad news that
C—— has lost his pastorate. I am not surprised.
He is courageous but tactless. Undoubtedly he
will regard himself as one of the Lord's martyrs.
Perhaps he is. Perhaps loyalty to principle will
always appear as tactlessness from the perspective of those who don't agree with you. But I
agree with C—— and still think him wanting
in common sense. At least he is pedagogically
very awkward.

You can't rush into a congregation which has
been fed from its very infancy on the individualistic ethic of Protestantism and which is immersed in a civilization where ethical individ-
ualism runs riot, and expect to develop a social
conscience among the people in two weeks. Nor
have you a right to insinuate that they are all
hypocrites just because they don't see what you
see.

Of course it is not easy to speak the truth
in love without losing a part of the truth, and
therefore one ought not be too critical of those
who put their emphasis on the truth rather than
on love. But if a man is not willing to try, at

least, to be pedagogical, and if in addition he
suffers from a martyr complex, he has no place
in the ministry. Undoubtedly there are more
ministers who violate their conscience than such
as suffer for conscience sake. But that is no
reason why those who have a robust conscience
should not try to master the pedagogical art.
Perhaps if they would learn nothing else but
to be less emotional and challenging in the pulpit and more informative and educational not
only in the pulpit but in their work with smaller
groups, they could really begin to change the
viewpoints and perspectives of their people.

1926

Spoke tonight to the Churchmen's Club of
———. The good Bishop who introduced me was
careful to disavow all my opinions before I
uttered them. He assured the brethren, however, that I would make them think. I am getting tired of these introductions which are intended to impress the speaker with the Christian virtue of the audience and its willingness
to listen to other than conventional opinions.
The chairman declares in effect, "Here is a
harebrained fellow who talks nonsense. But we
are Christian gentlemen who can listen with
patience and sympathy to even the most impossible opinions." It is just a device to destroy
the force of a message and to protect the sensitive souls who might be rudely shocked by a
religious message which came in conflict with
their interests and prejudices.

There is something pathetic about the timidity of the religious leader who is always afraid
of what an honest message on controversial
issues might do to his organization. I often
wonder when I read the eleventh chapter of
Hebrews in which faith and courage are prac-
tically identified whether it is psychologically

correct to assume that the one flows from the other. Courage is a rare human achievement. If it seems to me that preachers are more cowardly than other groups; that may be because I know myself. But I must confess that I haven't discovered much courage in the ministry. The average parson is characterized by suavity and circumspection rather than by any robust fortitude. I do not intend to be mean in my criticism because I am a coward myself and find it tremendously difficult to run counter to general opinion. Yet religion has always produced some martyrs and heroes.

I suppose religion in its most vital form does make men indifferent to popular approval. The apostle Paul averred that it was a small thing to be judged of men because he was seeking the approval of God. In a genuinely religious soul faith does seem to operate in that way. Issues are regarded *sub specie aeternitatis* and the judgment of contemporaries becomes insignificant. But the average man fashions his standards in the light of prevailing customs and opinions. It could hardly be expected that every religious leader would be filled with prophetic ardor and heedless courage. Many good men are naturally cautious. But it does seem that the unique resource of religion ought to give at least a touch of daring to the religious community and the religious leader.

1926

The excitement about the Federation of Labor convention in Detroit has subsided, but there are echoes of the event in various magazines. Several ministers have been commended for "courage" because they permitted labor leaders to speak in their churches who represented pretty much their own convictions and said pretty much what they had been saying for years.

It does seem pretty bad to have the churches lined up so solidly against labor and for the open shop policy of the town. The ministers are hardly to blame, except if they are to be condemned for not bringing out the meaning of Christianity for industrial relations more clearly in their ministry previous to the moment of crisis. As it was, few of the churches were sufficiently liberal to be able to risk an heretical voice in their pulpits. The idea that these A. F. of L. leaders are dangerous heretics is itself a rather illuminating clue to the mind of Detroit. I attended several sessions of the convention and the men impressed me as having about the same amount of daring and imagination as a group of village bankers.

The ministers of the country are by various methods dissociating themselves from the Detroit churches and are implying that they would have acted more generously in a like situation. Perhaps so. There are few cities in which wealth, suddenly acquired and proud of the mechanical efficiency which produced it, is so little mellowed by social intelligence. Detroit produces automobiles and is not yet willing to admit that the poor automata who are geared in on the production lines have any human problems.

Yet we differ only in degree from the rest of the country. The churches of America are on the whole thoroughly committed to the interests and prejudices of the middle classes. I think it is a bit of unwarranted optimism to expect them to make any serious contribution to the reorganization of society. I still have hopes that they will become sufficiently intelligent and heroic to develop some qualifying considerations in the great industrial struggle, but I can no longer envisage them as really determining factors in the struggle. Neither am I able for this reason to regard them as totally useless, as some of the critics do.

The ethical reconstruction of modern industrial society is, to be sure, a very important problem, but it is not the only concern of mankind. The spiritual amenities and moral decencies which the churches help to develop and preserve in the private lives of individuals are worth something for their own sake. Yet it must be obvious that if anyone is chosen by talent and destiny to put his life into the industrial struggle, the church is hardly his best vehicle.

The church is like the Red Cross service in war time. It keeps life from degenerating into a consistent inhumanity, but it does not materially alter the fact of the struggle itself. The Red Cross neither wins the war nor abolishes it. Since the struggle between those who have and those who have not is a never-ending one, society will always be, in a sense, a battleground. It is therefore of some importance that human loveliness be preserved outside of the battle lines. But those who are engaged in this task ought to realize that the brutalities of the conflict may easily negate the most painstaking humanizing efforts behind the lines, and that these efforts may become a method for evading the dangers and risks of the battlefield.

If religion is to contribute anything to the solution of the industrial problem, a more heroic type of religion than flourishes in the average church must be set to the task. I don't believe that the men who are driven by that kind of religion need to dissociate themselves from the churches, but they must bind themselves together in more effective association than they now possess.

1926

After preaching at —— University this morning I stopped off at —— and dropped in at the
Presbyterian church for the evening service.
The service was well attended and the music
was very good. The minister had a sermon
which might best be described as a fulsome
eulogy of Jesus Christ. I wonder whether sermons like that mean anything. He just piled up
adjectives. Every hero of ancient and modern
times was briefly described in order that he
might be made to bow before the superior virtue of the Lord. But the whole thing left me
completely cold. The superiority of Jesus was
simply dogmatically asserted and never adequately analyzed. There was not a thing in the
sermon that would give the people a clue to the
distinctive genius of Jesus or that would help
them to use the resources of his life for the
solution of their own problems.

Through the whole discourse there ran the
erroneous assumption that Christians are real
followers of Jesus and no effort was made to
describe the wide chasm which yawns between
the uncompromising idealism of the Galilean

and the current morality. I wonder how many sermons of that type are still being preached. If that sermon is typical it would explain much of the conventional tameness of the church.

How much easier it is to adore an ideal character than to emulate it.

1926

That resolution we passed in our pastors' meeting, calling upon the police to be more rigorous in the enforcement of law, is a nice admission of defeat upon the part of the church. Every one of our cities has a crime problem, not so much because the police are not vigilant as because great masses of men in an urban community are undisciplined and chaotic souls, emancipated from the traditions which guided their fathers and incapable of forming new and equally potent cultural and moral restraints. The children of the puritans are in this respect no better than the children of the immigrants. Both have reacted against traditions which do not fit their new circumstances and both are unable to escape license by new and better standards.

Perhaps the real reason that we live such chaotic lives in urban communities is because a city is not a society at all, and moral standards are formed only in societies and through the sense of mutual obligation which neighbors feel for one another. A big city is not a society held together by human bonds. It is a mass of individuals, held together by a productive process.

Its people are spiritually isolated even though
they are mechanically dependent upon one another. In such a situation it is difficult to create
and preserve the moral and cultural traditions
which each individual needs to save his life
from anarchy.

All of us do not live in moral chaos. But in
so far as we escape it, it is due to our loyalty
to religious, moral and cultural traditions which
have come out of other ages and other circumstances. That is why churches, Protestant, Catholic and Jewish, however irrelevant their ethical
idealism may be to the main facts of an industrial civilization, are nevertheless indispensable.
It is enough that our society should be morally
chaotic without also losing the kind of moral
restraint which still determines the life of many
individuals.

There is something very pathetic about the
efforts of almost every one of our large cities to
restore by police coercion what has been lost by
the decay of moral and cultural traditions. But
of course we do have to save ourselves from
anarchy, even if it must be done by force. Only
I think the church would do well to leave the
police problem alone. If violence must be used
temporarily, let the state do so without undue
encouragement from the church. The church
must work in another field and if it has failed

in that field, it cannot recoup its failures by giving advice to the police department. The priest as a sublimated policeman is a sorry spectacle.

1926

We were discussing the first commandment in the preparatory class today. The boys were trying to see whether "Thou shalt have no other Gods before me" meant anything in modern life. It is a constant source of surprise and delight to see with what profundity these boys and girls deal with the problems of life. They decided that anything that we loved more than God was in effect another god. But how do we love God, I asked. There were the usual answers which show how some children still identify religion with religious practices and customs, particularly Sunday observance. But one of of the boys came through with this answer, "We love God by loving the best we know." That seemed to me not bad at all.

Now we put on the blackboard all those interests which threatened to become gods to us: money, clothes (volunteered by a girl, of course), automobiles, eating, playing. We took up each one of these interests and tried to determine when they were in danger of becoming too central in life. On automobiles the boys didn't have much conscience except that they thought one ought not to clean them on Sunday. They take the cult of the automobile for granted as everyone else. The girls had quite a time defining the place where clothes cease to be a legitimate interest and become an obsession. I was probably a poor one to lead them in that discussion.

On the matter of eating there was considerable difficulty. "We have to eat to grow," said one of the boys. Correct answer. When then, is eating a form of idolatry? "When we eat all the time," suggested another boy. That left Junior in a corner. "I like to eat most all the time," he confessed ruefully. How can a hungry boy be anything but a sceptic about a philosophy of values which does not have eating at the center of it? Thus do the necessities of a robust organism defy the value schemes prompted by tradition or arrived at by reflection.

Junior just about stopped our discussion of comparative values by that confession, "I like to eat most all the time," and I couldn't help but think that my pedagogical impotence before this demand of natural life was closely akin to the impotence of the church before a youthful and vigorous national life, immersed in physical values and intent upon physical satisfactions. Our youthful nation is also declaring, "I love to eat most all the time"; and the error in its judgment is not easily overcome by preachment and precept until time and experience will show it the limits of animal satisfactions and teach it that man does not live by bread alone.

1926

I had a letter from a young preacher today who told me how he was suffering for truth's sake. He had merely been telling his congregation that Jesus was a great spiritual teacher, as was Confucius and Laotsze, and that the Christ idea was the product of Greek legend and ancient mythology. His good people were so ignorant, he thought, that they failed to show proper appreciation of his learning and resented his iconoclasm.

I find myself reacting violently to the sophomoric cocksureness of this young fellow. I suppose I am getting old and have made those compromises with the devil of superstition against which the editor of the Christian Register warns so hysterically. But for the life of me I can no more reduce Jesus to the status of a mere Galilean dreamer and teacher than I can accept the orthodox Christologies. The person who can make no distinction between a necessary symbolism and mythology seems to me no better than the wooden-headed conservative who insists that every bit of religious symbolism and

poetry must be accepted literally and meta-
physically.

It is not easy to define the God idea. Scientifically I suppose God is "the element of spirituality which is integral to reality," but for all
practical and religious purposes I find it both
helpful and justified to define him by saying that
"God is like Jesus." The ultimate nature of
reality cannot be grasped by science alone;
poetic imagination is as necessary as scientific
precision. Some of the supposedly ignorant peas-
ants against whom my youthful friend is drawing his heroic sword may have more truth on
their side than any fresh young theologue could
possibly realize.

1926

In the young men's class this morning we continued our discussion of the Sermon on the Mount. The boys have been making some interesting contributions. On the whole they are skeptical of the practicability of the demands which Jesus makes in the matter of trust and love and forgiveness. It is rather interesting to have this revelation of the basic cynicism of even the adolescent mind. They think that to follow Jesus "would put a business man out of business in no time," as one expressed it today. Of course, it is better to see the difficulties than to engage in some kind of sentimental avowal of Christian faith without realizing how stubbornly life resists the ideal.

After all, those boys are up against what St. Anthony saw when he was tempted by the vision of the young woman and the old woman. The one meant life but also lust, and the other meant faith but also death. At least that is the way Flaubert has it. It is certainly not easy to separate life from lust without destroying life. Yet Jesus came to give us a more abundant life.

"Maybe it would work if we tried it hard

enough," thought one of the boys today when
we discussed the practicability of trusting people. That may be the answer to the whole question.

1926

Bishop —— and I shared the platform tonight.
Fortunately, I spoke first so that I did not have
to compete with his powerful eloquence. His
sermon warmed the heart, but it was based upon
the uncritical assumption that modern Christianity is an exact replica of primitive Christianity
and is characterized by the same qualities of
heroism and faith. There was a disquieting
tendency to patronize in the good man's de-
meanor. I should think it would be a very difficult achievement for a bishop to be a real
Christian. The position is bound to aggravate the
inclination to pride which all of us possess. I do
not know many bishops intimately. The few that
I have known well have been singularly free of
arrogance; but they were unusual, for they were
saved by a sense of humor which is not frequently found in the pulpit and certainly hardly
ever in the episcopacy.

"Be not ye called rabbi," said Jesus, "and call
no man father upon earth, for one is your father
which is in heaven." I am not interested in applying the words of Jesus literally, but it seems to
me that the principle involved in these words

would wipe out the episcopacy. It wouldn't leave much justification either for "The Reverend Doctor." Of course the Christian community cannot do without leaders. But it might learn to save them from pride and arrogance.

The highest type of leadership maintains itself by its intrinsic worth, sans panoply, pomp and power. Of course, there are never enough real leaders to go around. Wherefore it becomes necessary to dress some men up and by other artificial means to give them a prestige and power which they could not win by their own resources. But it would be well if the church realized how dangerous power and prestige are, and how easily they corrupt a man's spiritual integrity.

It is certainly not to the credit of the church that it is less eager than the democratic state to circumscribe the authority and socialize the power of the leader. The Methodists try to preserve the proper spirit of humility among the bishops by relegating them to parliamentary impotence once every four years. But who wouldn't be willing to suffer for that brief period for the sake of the power and authority which the bishop exercises for the rest of the quadrennium?

Somewhere I read the observation of an anthropologist that naked savages could never have evolved a priesthood or an hereditary monarchy. No one is so much superior to his fellows that he deserves the positions of authority which a complex society finally evolves. That is why the leader must be put over with the proper clothes and paraphernalia. The throne and the crown make the king. Even the President of the United States has impressive naval and military aids to offset the unimposing frock which the democratic tradition prescribes. As for the bishop, who could be more awe-inspiring than a hierarch sitting upon his "throne" in his full regalia? That does not apply to Methodist bishops. But they have so much power that they don't need the panoply.

Think how insufferable bishops might be if they had to be both worshipped and feared. I am afraid that is true of Catholic bishops. Perhaps that is why the Catholic saints are not frequently found in the hierarchy.

1927

An impertinent youngster at the forum (mid-western college) accused me today of being an authoritarian because I quoted several modern philosophers and scientists in my address in support of my theistic belief. I made a deep bow before him and congratulated him upon being so proficient in laboratory experiments in every science and so profound in his philosophical meditations that he could arrive at his conclusions without the help of anyone else, scientist or philosopher.

His question did set me thinking on the problem of freedom. Why do we believe what we believe, and why do we do what we do? If the religion of my home had been harsh and unlovely I would probably be today where that young man is, in a position of rebellion against all religion. If I had not had the aid of this helpful professor and that illuminating book when my religious convictions were undergoing ad-justment I might not have made the necessary adjustments but would have thrown religious convictions into the discard.

If I were not in a position where human nature reveals itself in its more lovely characteristics would I be able to maintain confidence in the integity of man, upon which so much of the confidence in God depends? Has the class-conscious worker not a right to dismiss both my political and my religious convictions as bourgeois prejudices? And could I not with equal justice condemn his as myopic views which his resentments against society explain but do not prove true?

What we know as truth is determined by peculiar and individual perspectives. Pressures of environment, influences of heredity, and excellencies and deficiencies of teachers help to determine our life philosophies. We ought therefore to hold them with decent humility and a measure of scepticism. But if we permit ourselves to be tempted into a complete subjectivism and skepticism by these facts, we put an end to all philosophy and ultimately to civilization itself. For civilization depends upon the vigorous pursuit of the highest values by people who are intelligent enough to know that their values are qualified by their interests and corrupted by their prejudices.

1927

Perhaps there is no better illustration of the ethical impotence of the modern church than its failure to deal with the evils and the ethical problems of stock manipulation. Millions in property values are created by pure legerdemain. Stock dividends, watered stock and excessive rise in stock values, due to the productivity of the modern machine, are accepted by the church without a murmur if only a slight return is made by the beneficiaries through church philanthropies.

Here is C—— recapitalizing his business and adding six million dollars in stock. At least five of these millions will not be invested in physical expansion but pocketed by the owner. They simply represent capitalization of expected profits. Once this added burden has been placed upon the industry any demands of the workers for a larger share in the profits will be met by conclusive proof that the stock is earning only a small dividend and that further increase in wages would be "suicidal" to the business.

Meanwhile C—— has become quite philan-thropic. He gives fifty thousand dollars here and a hundred thousand there. Since the good man is a "Christian," religious organizations profit most by his benefactions. Every new donation is received with pæans of praise from church and press.

What I wonder is whether the gentleman is deceiving himself and really imagines himself a Christian or whether he is really quite hardboiled and harbors a secret contempt for the little men who buzz about his throne, singing their hallelujahs. One can never be sure how much we mortals are fooled by our own inadequate virtues and sanctified vices and how much we accept the world's convenient tribute without being convinced by it. Nor do I know which interpretation of the facts is to be preferred, not as a matter of truth, but as a matter of charity. What is worse—to be honest with yourself while you are dishonest with the world, or to be dishonest with the world because you have deceived yourself?

1927

Dropped in on the First —— Church of ——
on my way back from —— University. Went
into the young people's meeting before the
evening service and found a typical Endeavor
meeting in progress. Some ninety wholesome
youngsters were in attendance. All the various
tricks of a good Endeavor meeting were used.
Several little poems clipped from the Endeavor
World were recited at the appropriate time and
some of the members contributed quotations
from Scripture and from well-known authors.
The leader gave a good but platitudinous talk.
There was no discussion. My impression was that
this type of meeting, if still held, would be very
poorly attended. But here the facts belied my
theories. So much the worse for the young people of the church. Only a very inert type of
youngster could be satisfied with such a meeting, and only a very uncritical mind would
accept the pious platitudes which filled it, without uttering a protest or challenging a dozen
assumptions.

However much such meetings may cultivate
habits of loyalty to the church among young

people and preserve among them the traditional religious attitudes and customs, they do nothing to fit young people to live a Christian life amid the complexities of the modern world or to hold to the Christian faith in the perplexities of a scientific world view. What worries me particularly in regard to these meetings is the assumption which underlies them that nothing but moral good will is necessary to solve the problems of life. Almost every other meeting is a consecration meeting. No one seems to introduce the young people to the idea that an ethical life requires honest and searching intelligence. Nothing is done to discover to their eyes the tremendous chasm between the ideals of their faith and the social realities in which they live.

Under such circumstances we can expect no new vitality in the Christian life as the new generation takes hold. Old virtues and respectabilities will be maintained, but the areas of life which are still unchristian will remain as they are. I see the danger in our own discussion groups that the young people may satisfy all their idealism in incessant talk. But the talk has at least the merit of exploring all sides of a problem and of revealing the limitations of traditional attitudes and the need of new ventures in faith.

1927

Whenever I exchange thoughts with H——, as I do with greater frequency and with increasing profit to myself, I have the uneasy feeling that I belong to the forces which are destroying religion in the effort to refine it. He is as critical as I am—well, perhaps not quite so critical; but in all his critical evaluations of religious forms he preserves a robust religious vitality which I seem to lack. His scholarship is of course much more extensive than mine, but it has not robbed him of religious naïveté, to use Schweitzer's phrase. He has preserved a confidence in the goodness of men and the ultimate triumph of righteousness which I do not lack, but to which I do not hold so unwaveringly. While we understand each other, we really belong to different schools of thought.

I have been profoundly impressed by the Spenglerian thesis that culture is destroyed by the spirit of sophistication and I am beginning to suspect that I belong to the forces of decadence in which this sophistication is at work. I have my eye too much upon the limitations of contemporary religious life and institutions; I

always see the absurdities and irrationalities
in which narrow types of religion issue. That
wouldn't be so bad if I did not use the instru-
ments of intellectualism rather than those of a
higher spirituality for the critical task.

Nevertheless I hate a thoroughgoing cynic. I
don't want anyone to be more cynical than I am.
If I am saved from cynicism at all it is by some
sense of personal loyalty to the spirit and the
genius of Jesus; that and physical health. If I
were physically anæmic I never would be able
to escape pessimism. This very type of morbid
introspection is one of the symptoms of the disease. I can't justify myself in my perilous position except by the observation that the business of being sophisticated and naïve, critical
and religious, at one and the same time is as
difficult as it is necessary, and only a few are able
to achieve the balance. H—— says I lack a
proper appreciation of the mystical values in religion. That is probably the root of the matter.
Yet I can't resist another word in self-defense.
The modern world is so full of bunkum that it
is difficult to attempt honesty in it without an
undue emphasis upon the critical faculty.

If in this civilization we cannot enter the kingdom of God because we cannot be as little
children, the fault, dear Brutus, is in our stars
and not in ourselves.

1927

I fell in with a gentleman on the Pullman
smoker today (Pullman smokers are perfect in-
stitutes for plumbing the depths and shallows of
the American mind) who had made a killing
on the stock exchange. His luck appeared like
success from his perspective, and he was full of
the confidence with which success endows mortals. He spoke oracularly on any and all subjects.
He knew why the farmers were not making any
money and why the Europeans were not as
prosperous as we. Isn't it strange how gambler's
luck gives men the assurance of wisdom for
which philosophers search in vain? I pity this
man's wife. But she probably regards a new fur
coat as adequate compensation for the task of
appearing convinced by his obiter dicta.

1927

Seven clergymen sat down today with the national defense committee of the board of commerce. They invited us to talk over our stand against compulsory military education in the schools. It was an interesting experience, particularly as it came but shortly after our conflict with the same group on the matter of labor speakers in our pulpits. The contrasts in the attitude of the business men in these two controversies is very illuminating.

In the labor controversy they were hard-boiled realists who simply wanted to prevent labor from getting its side before the public. At that time they did not invite us to a round table discussion. They had nothing to discuss. They simply used their power in the city to prevent any discussion of the character of their power and the method of its preservation. In this case they were aggrieved and bewildered romanticists and idealists. They want military training in the schools because they have been told by the army officers that such training makes for patriotism. And patriotism is the only religion they know.

They invited us to a luncheon precisely because they felt themselves in a morally, not to say spiritually, impregnable position. I think they were quite sure that a little argument would convince us of the error of our ways. Our resistance was obviously very disconcerting to them. Perhaps they had a right to be disconcerted; for it is only a little while since there was a perfect alliance between the religion of patriotism and organized Christianity. Since most of the men do not attend church they had not heard of the qualms of conscience in the pulpit that had, at least for the time being, dissolved that alliance. We stood our ground and the meeting dissolved without any results.

I wonder if it isn't a little bit wicked to challenge the validity of the only kind of altruism which men know. But no—narrow loyalties may become more dangerous than selfishness.

1927

I wonder why it is that so many of the churches
which go in for vaudeville programs and the
hip-hip-hooray type of religious services should
belong to the Methodist and Baptist denominations. The vulgarities of the stunt preacher are
hardly compatible with either the robust spiritual vitality or the puritan traditions of the more
evangelistic churches. Perhaps the phenomenon
of which I speak is due merely to the size of
the two denominations. They may have more
showmen simply because they are big enough
to have more leaders of all varieties. Certainly
no church surpasses the Methodist in the number of men who possess real social passion and
imagination. Nor are the old emotionally warm
and naïvely orthodox preachers wanting in either
church.

Nevertheless there is a growing tendency toward stunt services in both denominations. Perhaps it represents the strategy of denominational
and congregational organisms which are too
much alive to accept the fate of innocuous des-
uetude, which has befallen some other churches.
Finding the masses, which they once attracted

by genuine religious emotion, less inclined to seek satisfaction in religion, they maintain themselves by offering such goods in entertainment and social life as the people seem to desire.

When the naïve enthusiasms of those generations, among whom religion is an emotional experience and not a social tradition, begin to cool, the churches which serve the new generations must either express religious feeling through devotion to moral and aesthetic values or they must substitute a baser emotionalism for the lost religious feeling. Perhaps the prevalence of cheap theatricality among the churches of our great democracy is a sign of the fact that the masses in America have lost the capacity for unreflective and exuberant religious feeling before they could acquire the kind of region which is closely integrated with the values of culture and art.

There is something pathetic about the effort of the churches to capture these spiritually vacuous multitudes by resort to any device which may intrigue their vagrant fancies. But it may not represent a total loss. The entertainment they offer may be vulgar, but it is not vicious, and without them the people might find satisfaction in something even cheaper.

1927

At the Lenten service today the dynamic speaker dilated upon the heroic character of the Christian faith. "Someone said to me recently," he reported, " 'Do you realize that it is dangerous to be a Christian?' 'Certainly,' I answered. 'It always has been and always will be.' "

Isn't it strange how we preachers insist on emphasizing the heroic aspect of the Christian faith? That pose today was exactly like the one struck by the minister in —— who loved to say dramatically, "The church needs a new casualty list," while it was generally known that he carefully evaded every issue which might create dissension or contention.

I think we ministers strike these heroic poses because we are dimly aware of the fact that the gospel commits us to positions which require heroic devotion before they will ever be realized in life. But we are astute rather than heroic and cautious rather than courageous. Thus we are in the dangerous position of being committed to the cross in principle but escaping it in practice. We are honest enough to be uneasy about that fact, but insincere enough to quiet our uneasiness by heroic poses.

Let any group of ministers gather and you will find someone declaring fervently, "No one ever tells me what to say. My congregation gives me perfect liberty." That is just another way of quieting an uneasy conscience; for we all know that if we explore the full meaning of a gospel of love its principles will be found to run counter to cherished prejudices. It is of course not impossible to retain freedom of the pulpit, but if anyone is doing so without the peril of defections from his ranks and opposition to his message, he is deceiving himself about the quality of his message. Either his message is too innocuous to deserve opposition or too conventional to arouse it.

An astute pedagogy and a desire to speak the truth in love may greatly decrease opposition to a minister's message and persuade a difficult minority to entertain at least, and perhaps to profit by, his message; but if a gospel is preached without opposition it is simply not the gospel which resulted in the cross. It is not, in short, the gospel of love.

1927

Talked today at the open forum which meets every Sunday afternoon in the high school. The "lunatic fringe" of the city congregates there, in addition to many sensible people. The question period in such meetings is unfortunately monopolized to a great extent by the foolish ones, though not always. Today one old gentleman wanted to know when I thought the Lord would come again, while a young fellow spoke volubly on communism and ended by challenging me to admit that all religion is fantasy. Between those two you have the story of the tragic state of religion in modern life. One half of the world seems to believe that every poetic symbol with which religion must deal is an exact definition of a concrete or an historical fact; the other half, having learned that this is not the case, can come to no other conclusion but that all religion is based upon fantasy.

Fundamentalists have at least one characteristic in common with most scientists. Neither can understand that poetic and religious imagination has a way of arriving at truth by giving a clue to the total meaning of things without be-

ing in any sense an analytic description of detailed facts. The fundamentalists insist that religion is science, and thus they prompt those
who know that this is not true to declare that
all religious truth is contrary to scientific fact.

How can an age which is so devoid of poetic
imagination as ours be truly religious?

1927

Our city race commission has finally made its report after months of investigation and further months of deliberation on our findings. It has been a rare experience to meet with these white and colored leaders and talk over our race problems. The situation which the colored people of the city face is really a desperate one, and no one who does not spend real time in gathering the facts can have any idea of the misery and pain which exists among these people, recently migrated from the south and unadjusted to our industrial civilization. Hampered both by their own inadequacies and the hostility of a white world they have a desperate fight to keep body and soul together, to say nothing of developing those amenities which raise life above the brute level.

I wish that some of our romanticists and sentimentalists could sit through a series of meetings where the real social problems of a city are discussed. They would be cured of their optimism. A city which is built around a productive process and which gives only casual thought and incidental attention to its human problems is really a kind of hell. Thousands in this town are really living in torment while the rest of us eat, drink and make merry. What a civilization!

Incidentally I wish the good church people who hate our mayor so much because he doesn't conform to their rules and standards could appreciate how superior his attitudes and viewpoints on race relations are to those held by most church people. It seems to me rather unfortunate that we must depend upon the "publicans" for our social conscience to so great a degree while the "saints" develop their private virtues and let the city as such fry in its iniquities.

1927

I think I have solved the Sunday night service problem for good. I give a short address or sermon upon a more or less controversial moral issue, or upon a perplexing religious question, and after closing the service we have a half-hour to forty-five minutes of discussion. The group attracted by this kind of program is not large. It is not the usual forum crowd. But it is a group of unusually thoughtful people, and the way they explore the fundamental themes and problems of life is worth more than many sermons.

I am absolutely convinced that such discussions come to grips with life's real problems much more thoroughly than any ex cathedra utterance from the pulpit. For one thing the people themselves make the application of general principles to specific experiences. Then, too, they inevitably explore the qualifications which life seems to make upon every seemingly absolute principle. The real principles of Christian living seem so much more real and also so much more practicable when a group of thoughtful people make an honest effort to fit them into the complexities of modern life.

Perhaps the most interesting point about such a discussion is the way every type of experience can be used to illustrate a certain general truth. Last Sunday night an advertising man made a most interesting contribution to the question of marriage and divorce out of his experience as advertising counsel. He said that he had learnt in business that it is always well to regard relationships as permanent even when they are not so absolutely in a legal sense. If the parties to a contract assume that it can be broken easily they will not extend themselves as they ought to make those adjustments which a permanent relationship requires.—Thus we make the experience gained in one field of activity serve the problem of another field. Again and again thoughtful mothers have thrown light upon the problems of democracy, the place of coercion in life and the efficacy of trust out of experience gained in their work with their children.

If there were only more thoughtful people it would be worth while to change every service into something like this evening discussion. But discussion requires time and it doesn't mean much to people who are looking for "inspiration" rather than guidance. I suppose there is still a place for inspirational addresses. But in a world in which so many traditional moral ideas are in solution and so many others are generally accepted and never applied, this kind of honest searching with others, rather than for them, is particularly rewarding.

1927

I wonder if it is really possible to have an honest
Thanksgiving celebration in an industrial civilization. Harvest festivals were natural enough
in peasant communities. The agrarian feels himself dependent upon nature's beneficence and
anxious about nature's caprices. When the au-
tumnal harvest is finally safe in the barns there
arise, with the sigh of relief, natural emotions
of gratitude that must express themselves reli-
giously, since the bounty is actually created by
the mysterious forces of nature which man may
guide but never quite control.

All that is different in an industrial civilization in which so much wealth is piled up by the
ingenuity of the machine, and, at least seemingly, by the diligence of man. Thanksgiving
becomes increasingly the business of congratu-
lating the Almighty upon his most excellent co-
workers, ourselves. I have had that feeling about
the Thanksgiving proclamations of our Presi-
dents for some years. An individual, living in an
industrial community might still celebrate a
Thanksgiving day uncorrupted by pride, because he does benefit from processes and forces

which he does not create or even guide. But a national Thanksgiving, particularly if it is meant to express gratitude for material bounty, becomes increasingly a pharisaic rite.

The union Thanksgiving service we attended this morning was full of the kind of self-righteous bunk which made it quite impossible for me to worship. There was indeed a faint odor of contrition in one of the prayers and in an aside of the sermon, but it did not spring from the heart. The Lord who was worshipped was not the Lord of Hosts, but the spirit of Uncle Sam, given a cosmic eminence for the moment which the dear old gentleman does not deserve.

It is a bad thing when religion is used as a vehicle of pride. It would be better to strut unashamedly down the boardwalk of nations than to go through the business of bowing humbly before God while we say, "We thank thee Lord that we are not as other men."

1927

Mother and I visited at the home of —— today where the husband is sick and was out of employment before he became sick. The folks have few connections in the city. They belong to no church. What a miserable existence it is to be friendless in a large city. And to be dependent upon a heartless industry. The man is about 55 or 57 I should judge, and he is going to have a desperate time securing employment after he gets well. These modern factories are not meant for old men. They want young men and they use them up pretty quickly. Your modern worker, with no skill but what is in the machine, is a sorry individual. After he loses the stamina of youth, he has nothing to sell.

I promised —— I would try to find him a job. I did it to relieve the despair of that family, but I will have a hard time making good on my promise. According to the ethics of our modern industrialism men over fifty, without special training, are so much junk. It is a pleasure to see how such an ethic is qualified as soon as the industrial unit is smaller and the owner has a personal interest in his men. I could mention quite a few such instances. But unfortunately the units are getting larger and larger and more inhuman.

I think I had better get in contact with more of these victims of our modern industrialism and not leave that end of our work to mother alone. A little such personal experience will help much to save you from sentimentality.

1927

Have just returned from the student conference at ——. A smart young professor told the students that all social customs are based upon irrational taboos. Our generation is the first with the opportunity to build a rational social order. The way to build a rational society, according to this savant, is to regard every relationship, custom, convention and law as irrational until it has proved itself rational by experience.

A sample of the kind of society he would build by his reason was given in his discussion of sex relations. He thinks the highest kind of family life would result from the love of one woman for one man while both indulged in promiscuous relations. Thus would the values of both freedom and love be maintained. The smart young man seems never to have heard that you cannot have your cake and eat it too.

If you want love and cooperation in any kind of society, and most of all in the family, it is necessary to sacrifice some freedom for its sake. What strange fanatics these moderns are! Imagining themselves dispassionate in their evaluation of all values, they are really bigoted pro-

tagonists of the one value of freedom. Every
other value must be subordinated to it.

It is true that every convention, custom, law
and usage contains an irrational element. Some
were unreasonable from the beginning and
others have become so by shifting circumstance.
It is necessary, therefore, that we approach the
facts of life experimentally and scientifically,
rather than traditionally. However, it seems to
me quite unreasonable to proceed upon the assumption that all traditions are wholly unreasonable. Most of the moderns who think so are
significantly defective in the knowledge of history.

There is at the heart of almost every tradition
an element of reasonableness and around its cir-
cumference a whole series of irrationalities. Our
business must be to destroy the latter and restore the former by fitting it to contemporaneous circumstances and conditions.

I doubt whether it is wise for every person to
be extremely critical of all traditions in every
field of thought and life. I imagine we ought to
specialize a little in this matter and let various
people experiment in various areas. This seems
to me a wise policy for the simple reason that
it does not make for happiness for one person to
do the experimenting in every field. At any rate
most of the intellectuals I know who try to do

it are miserable souls. I am always glad to escape their company and consort with folks who take some things for granted. There is an unnatural strain in their lives and, having made a virtue of the critical temper, they usually discount virtue and achievement even where it is indubitable.

Since there are many more traditionalists than experimentalists, all this may be bad advice. But I doubt whether the lethargy of the many justifies the few in spoiling their tempers and their judgment. Let every reformer find at least one field of interest and life where he can be happily conventional. If he is trying to remake the economic order, let him accept family life and be happy in it without too many scruples about its alleged imperfections. On second thought I don't like this advice. At any rate it is inconsistent with my scorn for the liberal theologians who are so preoccupied with the task of reforming religion that they have no interest in the iniquities of society which ought to challenge their conscience.

Let us have reformers, then, who try to reform everything at the same time! But I am going to keep my distance from them.

1927

The new Ford car is out. The town is full of talk about it. Newspaper reports reveal that it is the topic of the day in all world centers. Crowds storm every exhibit to get the first glimpse of this new creation. Mr. Ford has given out an interview saying that the car has cost him about a hundred million dollars and that after finishing it he still has about a quarter of a billion dollars in the bank.

I have been doing a little arithmetic and have come to the conclusion that the car cost Ford workers at least fifty million in lost wages during the past year. No one knows how many hundreds lost their homes in the period of unemployment, and how many children were taken out of school to help fill the depleted family exchequer, and how many more children lived on short rations during this period. Mr. Ford refuses to concede that he made a mistake in bringing the car out so late. He has a way of impressing the public even with his mistakes. We are now asked to believe that the whole idea of waiting a year after the old car stopped selling before bringing out a new one was a great advertising

scheme which reveals the perspicacity of this
industrial genius. But no one asks about the
toll in human lives.

What a civilization this is! Naïve gentlemen
with a genius for mechanics suddenly become
the arbiters over the lives and fortunes of hundreds of thousands. Their moral pretensions are
credulously accepted at full value. No one both-
ers to ask whether an industry which can maintain a cash reserve of a quarter of a billion
ought not make some provision for its unem-
ployed. It is enough that the new car is a good
one. Here is a work of art in the only realm of
art which we can understand. We will therefore
refrain from making undue ethical demands
upon the artist. Artists of all the ages have been
notoriously unamenable to moral discipline.
The cry of the hungry is drowned in the song,
"Henry has made a lady out of Lizzy."

1927

This prayer book controversy in the Church of England ought to give us liberals who make so much of tolerance a pause. What are the limits of tolerance? Does not tolerance of a theological position which one knows or believes to be untrue become a betrayal of the truth? How can one be tolerant of medievalism without playing traitor to the best in the modern day?

Here is the Episcopal church which many of us have counted blessed because it was the one bridge over the chasm which separates Catholicism and Protestantism. But the chasm is now revealed as too wide for any bridge. Cooperation with the Catholic demands connivance with religious practices which reduce religion to magic. No wonder the Protestant laymen in Parliament threw the revised prayer book out. How can anyone in the year of our Lord 1927 be seriously exercised over the problem of the "real presence" in the Eucharist? Think of the spiritual leaders of a torn and bleeding world debating learnedly on whether and how God can be magically localized and salvation be confined in a capsule. To read the arguments of the sacerdotalists is enough to drive one into the arms of the unrepentant rationalists who regard all religion as dangerous.

The weaknesses of Catholicism ought not prompt one to disregard all the finer spiritual and moral values which still live in this ancient church. But there can be no final unity between an institution which reduces religion to magic and a fellowship of the spirit which tries to subdue the chaos of life under the ideal of faith.

Magic is an enemy of all morality. It offers a short cut to all prizes of the spirit which can be won only by heroic effort.

1927

After speaking at ——— University today Professor ——— said he objected to my assumption that the family is the root of human societies. He said he believed that most forms of human cooperation were formed by men who had to resist the special interests of the family, as typified particularly by the narrow loyalty of the mother to her own offspring, before they could establish wider fellowships. That was a new idea to me and one that seems to be not without merit. Of course it does not invalidate the thesis that the family is the first unit of society; for the first fighting unit was probably composed of a group of fathers and sons and sons' sons. That is, not the family in the narrowest but in the widest sense, the family as it develops into the clan is the first real society.

The idea that the family is frequently opposed to ventures in wider fellowship is justified by more than one present fact. The family is still essentially selfish, and many a man is beguiled from ideal ventures by a false sense of obligation to his family. Think of the number of men who sell their souls merely that their wives and children may enjoy higher standards of living than other families. Think of the number of mothers whose interest in life never goes beyond the ambition to secure special advantages for their children. The mother of the sons of Zebedee is a good example. In her you have motherhood in its tragic limitations as well as in its sublime beauty.

The family is not inevitably selfish or invariably opposed to larger ventures in fellowship, but it may easily become so. Jesus' ruthless words, "He who loveth father or mother more than me is not worthy of me, he who loveth son and daughter more than me is not worthy of me," have more meaning than most Christians have realized. Celibacy may be wrong because it escapes rather than solves this problem. But the invariable tendency of religious movements of great moral sensitiveness to experiment with celibacy is significant. Thus speaks a bachelor. Let the cynic make the most of the private prejudice which colors this judgment.

1928

This conference on religious education seems to your humble servant the last word in absurdity. We are told by a delightful "expert" that we ought not really teach our children about God lest we rob them of the opportunity of making their own discovery of God, and lest we corrupt their young minds by our own superstitions. If we continue along these lines the day will come when some expert will advise us not to teach our children the English language, since we rob them thereby of the possibility of choosing the German, French or Japanese languages as possible alternatives. Don't these good people realize that they are reducing the principle of freedom to an absurdity?

Religion, like language, is a social product. The potentialities for both are in the child, but their highest articulations are the result of ages of cultural and spiritual experience, and in the right kind of religious education the experience of the race is joined with the inclinations of the individual. We do not get a higher type of religious idealism from children merely by with-

holding our own religious ideas from them
(however they may be filled with error), any
more than we would get a higher type of civilization by letting some group of youngsters shift
for themselves upon a desert island.

A wise architect observed that you could
break the laws of architectural art provided you
had mastered them first. That would apply to
religion as well as to art. Ignorance of the past
does not guarantee freedom from its imperfections. More probably it assures the repetition of
past errors. We ought of course to cultivate a
wholesome scepticism in our young people so
that they will not accept the ideas of the past
too slavishly. But appreciation must come before criticism.

We do not teach a child the limitations of
Beethoven before we have helped it to appreciate him; nor do we withhold any appreciation
of the classics in order that the child might be
free to prefer Stravinsky to Beethoven. What
some of these moderns are doing is simply to
destroy the organs of religious insight and the
atmosphere in which religious attitudes may
flourish, ostensibly for the sake of freedom, but
really at its expense.

I have a dark suspicion that some of these
modern religious educators do not really know

what religion is about. They want a completely rational faith and do not realize that they are killing religion by a complete rationalization. With all their pious phraseology and supposedly modern pedagogy they really are decadent forces.

Life is a battle between faith and reason in which each feeds upon the other, drawing sustenance from it and destroying it. Nature has wisely ordained that faith shall have an early advantage in the life of the child to compensate for its later difficulties. If we imagine that we help the progress of the race by inoculating children with a premature sophistication we are of all men most miserable. Reason, without the balance of faith, destroys a civilization soon enough, without giving it this advantage among the young. I wonder if any of these modern religious pedagogues have ever read Unamuno's *The Tragic Sense of Life?*

Here I am talking like a fundamentalist. But why not? If we must choose between types of fanaticism is there any particular reason why we should prefer the fanatics who destroy a vital culture in the name of freedom and reason to those who try to strangle a new culture at birth in the name of authority and dogma? The latter type of fanaticism is bound to end in futility.

The growth of reason cannot be stopped by
dogma. But the former type is dangerous because it easily enervates a rational culture wit!
ennui and despair.

1928

This Federal Council meeting is an interesting study in the geography of morals. The race commission presented a report today in which it tried to place the council on record as favoring the enforcement of the fifteenth amendment as well as the eighteenth. It was obviously an effort to exploit the strong prohibition sentiment of the churches for the sake of committing them to the espousal of the interests of the disfranchised Negroes in the south. That is not a bad political strategy. But it did not quite work.

A good brother from the southern Presbyterian church warned that to interfere with this "political issue" would "soil the garments of the bride of Christ." To him the eighteenth amendment represented a "moral" issue but the fifteenth was a "political" one. I have a sneaking suspicion that the fifteenth amendment expresses more of the genius of the gospel than the eighteenth, but that is neither here nor there. What was interesting was the way in which various church leaders tried to rescue us from the embarrassment into which the council was brought by this proposal.

A good brother who was raised in the south and now lives in the north tried to act as mediator. He introduced his remarks with the usual nice story about how much he loved his Negro mammy. Some day he ought to have a lesson in ethics and learn how much easier it is to love those who acknowledge their inferiority than those who challenge our superiority. It is indeed a virtuous woman who can love her social competitor as sincerely as she loves her faithful maid.

Another mediator was a southern bishop who has many northern connections. He made much of the fact that the south disregards only the spirit and not the letter of the enfranchising amendments to the constitution. The bishop is really a man of some courage who has spoken out bravely on the industrial conditions in the south. But he was evidently afraid in this instance either to accept or to reject a Christian view of race relations. So he stuck to casuistry about the letter of the law. He has probably preached many a sermon on the text about the letter killing and the spirit making alive. At any rate everyone who spoke revealed how geographic and historical circumstance had qualified Christian conviction.

That was as true of those of us who took an uncompromising position as the southern equiv-

ocators and the semi-southern mediators. To
the southerners we are not Christian idealists
but merely "Yankee" meddlers. And perhaps we
are. At any rate it was easy to see from the debate that the north cannot help the south much
in solving its race problem. If it is solved the
solution must come out of the conscience and
heart of the south.

After all, the problem, as every moral problem, is not merely conditioned by geography
but by mathematics. Contact between races
when the one race is almost as numerous as the
other is quite a different story from a relationship in which the subject race is numerically
very much weaker than the dominant group.
Therefore let us not judge, lest we be judged.
It is so easy to repent of other people's sins.

Nevertheless it does not make one feel very
comfortable to have a great church body seek
some politic solution for a problem in which the
ideal of Christian brotherhood leaves little room
for equivocation.

1928

There is a discouraging pettiness about human nature which makes me hate myself each time I make an analysis of my inner motives and springs of action. Here I am prodding and criticizing people continually because they have made too many compromises with the necessities of life and adjusted the Christian ideal until it has completely lost its original meaning. Yet I make my own compromises all the time.

It is Christian to trust people, and my trust is carefully qualified by mistrust and caution.

It is Christian to love, and to trust in the potency of love rather than in physical coercion. Logically that means non-resistance. Yet I believe that a minimum of coercion is necessary in all social tasks, or in most of them.

It is Christian to forgive rather than to punish; yet I do little by way of experimenting in the redemptive power of forgiveness.

I am not really a Christian. In me, as in many others, "the native hue of resolution is sicklied o'er by a pale cast of thought." I am too cautious to be a Christian. I can justify my caution, but so can the other fellow who is more cautious than I am.

The whole Christian adventure is frustrated continually not so much by malice as by cowardice and reasonableness. Of course everyone must decide for himself just where he is going to put his peg; where he is going to arrive at some stable equilibrium between moral adventure and necessary caution. And perhaps everyone is justified if he tries to prove that there is a particular reasonableness about the type of compromise which he has reached. But he might well learn, better than I have learned, to be charitable with those who have made their adjustments to the right and to the left of his position. If I do not watch myself I will regard all who make their adjustments to my right as fanatics and all who make them to the left as cowards. There is a silly egotism about such an attitude. But it is difficult to be pedagogically effective if you do not hold pretty resolutely to some position.

A reasonable person adjusts his moral goal somewhere between Christ and Aristotle, between an ethic of love and an ethic of moderation. I hope there is more of Christ than of Aristotle in my position. But I would not be too sure of it.

1928

Jack Hyde came up today for a chat. These
newspaper men are always interesting company.
As religious editor of the Daily ——, he has
been following the preachers of the town pretty
closely. Of course he is a cynic, though a gentle
one. He tells many an interesting story on how
the preachers try to get free publicity.

I think there ought to be a club in which
preachers and journalists could come together
and have the sentimentalism of the one matched
with the cynicism of the other. That ought to
bring them pretty close to the truth. The interesting part of the contrast is that the newspaper
is officially as optimistic about contemporary
life as the pulpit. The difference between the
two is that the preacher is ensnared by his own
sentimentality and optimism while the newspaper man has two views, one for official and one
for private consumption.

1928

My good friend —— has sent me his church calendar. Among other things he reports "Last Sunday almost as many strangers as members were present. The weather was a bit cold. Was your loyalty chilly too? You cannot fight battles with half the soldiers in their tents. Lent is here. Give your church the right of way. Do your duty next Sunday."

Here we see how easily even the Protestant minister gravitates to the viewpoint of the priest. He thinks people ought to regard it as a duty to hear him preach. What is still worse is that he identifies church attendance with moral heroism. Does he not realize that faithful church attendance develops and reveals the virtue of patience much more than the virtue of courage?

I must admit that I have urged people to come to church myself as a matter of duty. But I can do so no longer. The church service is not an end in itself. Not even religion is an end in itself. If the church service does not attract people by the comfort and challenge it brings to them, we only postpone the evil day if we compel attendance by appealing to their sense of duty. It may not be wrong to appeal to their sense of loyalty to the institution and tell them that if they have identified themselves with the institution as members they owe it to the strangers to be there. But even that is dangerous. The church is already too much an end in itself.

These appeals make it appear that we regard religious devotion as a service to God, a very dangerous idea. Of course a modern preacher doesn't really believe that. What is really in his mind, consciously or unconsciously, is that the people owe him the duty to hear him preach. That is perhaps a natural glorification of his own function but it cannot be denied that there is something pathetic about it.

I can see, of course, that all good things depend in part upon right habits. Customs, attitudes and actions which are desirable cannot always depend upon impulse and will. It may be a good thing that people attend church as a matter of habit and because of a general sense of obligation to the institution. If churches depended only upon people who must make up their minds each Sunday whether or no they will attend church, our attendance would be even smaller than it is.

Yet habitual actions easily become meaningless, and institutions which depend upon them

lose their vitality. If habitual actions are not
continually revitalized by the compulsion of
ideals and the attraction of the values involved
in them, they may easily become useless.

1928

Detroit observed Good Friday today as never before. Sixteen theatres and many churches besides were filled to capacity during the three-hour period. I wonder how one is to understand this tremendous devotion of this pagan city. How little place the real spirit of Christ has in the industrial drive of this city. And yet men and women flock by the thousands to meditate upon the cross. Perhaps we are all like the centurian who helped to crucify Jesus and then was so impressed by the whole drama of the cross that the confession was forced from his lips "Surely this was the son of God."

Before going to the theatre service I passed a Methodist church with a message on its bulletin board that explains many chapters in American church history. It was: "Good Friday service this afternoon. Snappy song service." So we combine the somber notes of religion with the jazz of the age.

I wonder if anyone who needs a snappy song service can really appreciate the meaning of the cross. But perhaps that is just a Lutheran prejudice of mine.

1928

A very sophisticated young man assured me in our discussion today (student discussion at a middle western university) that no intelligent person would enter the ministry today. He was sure that the ministry was impossible as a vocation not only because too many irrationalities were still enmeshed with religion but also because there was no real opportunity for usefulness in the church. I tried to enlighten this sophomoric wise man.

Granted all the weaknesses of the church and the limitations of the ministry as a profession, where can one invest one's life where it can be made more effective in as many directions?

You can deal with children and young people and help them to set their life goals and organize their personalities around just and reasonable values.

You can help the imperiled family shape the standards and the values by which the institution of family life may be saved and adjusted to the new conditions of an industrial civilization.

You can awaken a complacent civilization to

the injustices which modern industrialism is developing. While ministers fail most at this point there is nothing to prevent a courageous man from making a real contribution to his society in this field.

You can soften the asperities of racial conflict and aid the various groups of a polyglot city to understand one another and themselves.

You can direct the thoughts and the hopes of men to those facts and those truths which mitigate the cruelty of the natural world and give men the opportunity to assert the dignity of human life in the face of the contempt of nature.

You can help them to shape and to direct their hopes and aspirations until their lives are determined and molded by the ideal objects of their devotion. While it is true that magic and superstition are still entwined, seemingly inextricably intertwined, with the highest hopes and assurances of mankind, you may find real joy as a skillful craftsman in separating hopes from illusions so that the one need not perish with the other.

Here is a task which requires the knowledge of a social scientist and the insight and imagination of a poet, the executive talents of a business man and the mental discipline of a philosopher. Of course none of us meets all the demands made upon us. It is not easy to be all things to all men. Perhaps that is why people are so critical of us. Our task is not specific enough to make a high degree of skill possible or to result in tangible and easily measured results. People can find fault with us easily enough and we have no statistics to overawe them and to negate their criticisms.

1928

I spoke today at the "Victory dinner" of one of our civic organizations which had been conducting a financial campaign in the interest of its worthy objects. Not being well prepared I animadverted disconnectedly upon the lack of culture in Detroit and expressed the hope that the dawn of a new day was breaking.

Mr. —— who sat close to me was so angry about what I said that he confessed that he had been tempted to interrupt me in the middle of my address. He cited a large benefaction of his in the interest of a religious organization as proof of Detroit's culture and insisted that the "old families," to which he belonged, had real culture, whatever might be said about the newer crowd. I told him his contribution was in the interest of righteousness rather than culture. Inasmuch as it is generally known that he made a fortune by rigging the stock market, he was a little nonplussed by my answer. We finally came to an amicable agreement upon the proposition that the streets of Detroit are cleaner than those of Chicago.

1928

I believe every preacher ought to take several radical journals, preferably the ones which are extremely inimical to religion. The ethical ideals of Christianity are so high and the compromises which the average church and the average minister has made between these ideals and the economic necessities of society are so great, and self-deception is so easy, that we need the corrective of a critical and perhaps cynical evaluation of religion in modern life.

I should like to recommend this kind of reading particularly to successful ministers who are so easily obsessed by a messianic complex because of the compliments they receive. Let them remind themselves that there are astute observers who think that all their preaching is superficial and never touches the fundamental defects of modern society, and that these critics are at least as near the truth as their too generous devotees.

1928

I think I ought to repent of the many unkind things I have said about various ministers. We liberal preachers (I am thinking of social liberalism now) are too ready to attribute conventional opinions to cowardice. What we don't realize is that the great majority of parsons simply don't share our radical convictions. If they get along very handsomely in the kind of a civilization in which we live, that is simply because they are in sincere general agreement with the prevailing ideas of our day. Of course I think we have a right to wonder a little how one can claim discipleship to one who disturbed history so much and yet be such a thorough conformist. Yet it is usually not cowardice but mental inertia which creates the conformity; and sometimes the conformity is the honest fruit of a finely poised rather than a daring mind. After all most of us are conformists in some sense, and it is rather presumptuous on our part to condemn every type of conformity except our own.

I am moved to this reflection by the insistence of such men as the editor of the Christian Register that every liberal who remains in an evangelical communion and does not immediately join the Unitarian church must be prompted by cowardice. When it is theological rather than social liberalism that is made the test of conformity or radicalism, it is my ox that is gored, and I begin to recant my previous harsh opinions. If the editor of the Register can go so far wrong in gauging the motives of evangelical liberals we social radicals may be wrong in explaining why parsons fail to be thoroughgoing pacifists. Great achievement! I learn how to be tolerant when I become the victim of somebody else's spiritual pride.

1928

Had a profitable talk with a Jewish friend in the east. He said the only Christian church that he could ever join would be that of the Quakers. Of course he would not join the Quakers in the kind of a world in which we are living, where Christians practice social ostracism against Jews and thereby force every Jew to regard such a transfer of religious loyalty in the light of treason to his racial community. He felt that if he were free to choose his religious group he would choose the Quakers because they have no professional ministry. He dabbles in psychiatry and thinks he has looked through the professional minister.

I would like to have him talk to a group of preachers sometime. Like all realists he barely escapes the kind of cynicism which destroys wholesome human relations. But he does escape it and is not at all bitter in his analysis of human nature. That is why his reaction to the ministry disquiets me. He has his hands on considerable truth.

There is something very artificial about the professional ministry. When religion deals with

magic the professional priests can dispense the
magic and be quite happy. But when religion
becomes a search for all of life's highest values
there is something incongruous about making
your living in the business of helping people to
discover and develop these values. I don't think
this consideration invalidates the ministry as a
profession. In a day of specialists and experts
there ought to be room for a specialist in moral
and spiritual values. But think of commanding
a large salary because you are a better preacher
than someone else! Isn't that putting a market
value on the ability of a man to help people find
God? Fortunately it is the rhetorical rather than
the spiritual gift that usually creates the different prices in the preacher market.

1928

Passing one of our big churches today I ran across this significant slogan, calculated to impress the passing wayfarer: "We Will Go Out of Business. When? When Every Man in Detroit Has Been Won to Christ." Of course it is just a slogan and not to be taken too seriously, but the whole weakness of Protestantism is in it. Here we are living in a complex world in which thousands who have been "won to Christ" haven't the slightest notion how to live a happy life or how to live together with other people without making each other miserable.

Yet the church goes about the business of winning people to Christ — that is, pulling them through some kind of emotional or social experience in which they are made to commit themselves, or in which they really do commit themselves, to the good life as it is symbolized in Christ, and imagining that this is the end of the task. I do not say that such commitments do not have their value. But surely one must be very blind to live under the illusion that the desire or even the will to live a Christ-life is automatically fulfilled in present-day society or in any society.

The church which conceived that slogan is really better than the silly advertisement might lead one to suppose. I think people receive some light and leading there. Nevertheless, most of its energies go into the business of "winning others."

The saddest part about these highly evangelistic churches who put everything into the recruiting task is that they generally tempt those who are already "won" to imagine themselves perfect, or at least "saved." I know one lawyer in that church, and not a bad man either, who needs to be "won" to several ideas in the gospel of Christ about which he hasn't the faintest glimmer of light. But he is too sure of himself to get a new idea.

1928

Here is a minister making a confession in his weekly paper: "Last Sunday night," he writes, "I was at my worst and unfortunately there were many strangers in the audience. I tried, but I could not get the ball over the plate. I had taught a Sunday-school class, preached over the radio, gone out to dinner, entertained a guest at supper, met the —— committee and failed to get rest after Easter. I will try to do better next Sunday, so come then."

It is all very nice and humble, but there is an implication of professionalism in the whole thing that is appalling. The idea is that he didn't put on a good performance, "didn't get the ball over the plate." There you have the whole weakness of a professional ministry, striving each Sunday to make an interesting speech. It simply can't be denied that the business of furnishing inspiration twice each week, on a regular schedule, by a person who is paid to do just that and whose success is judged by the amount of "pep" he can concentrate in his homilies, is full of moral and spiritual dangers. To follow such a program without running into spiritual bankruptcy requires the resources of a saint.

1928

Arriving at —— today, I was put up at the luxurious home of a very charming potentate of the local pulpit. I was driven to my meeting in a big Packard car (a gift of the congregation, my host informed me) with a liveried chauffeur at the wheel. I don't think I would have reacted so strongly against this kind of life if I hadn't been reading Savotorelli's *Life of St. Francis* on the way down and was inclined to look at the world through the little brother's rather than my own eyes.

To object to this kind of luxury for ministers, and not voice the same objection in regard to the standards of living among laymen, may seem to involve us in a moral dualism. But I am no longer afraid of dualism. We might well have more of it. It will be a long while before we can convince laymen of the spiritual implications in standards of living in a civilization which knows of no other way to give a man a sense of achievement than to let him advertise it by outward show. But ministers ought to know better.

Furthermore there is a moral peril in accept-

ing the largess of men to whom you are trying
to minister. It is not that they try to take conscious advantage of your sense of gratitude,
but that such dependence upon their generosity
creates a psychological hazard against honest
presentation of the truth. Of course it is probably true that men who receive these excessive
benefactions are usually too tame to need tam-
ing. Innocuous virtue is always more charming
and more liable to prompt a generous affection
than the kind which raises disquieting questions.

Then too, ministers who can preach the gospel of Jesus in our kind of civilization without
making anyone uncomfortable deserve an automobile for the difficult feat. And they need one
to compensate them for that lack of spiritual
vitality which makes the performance of the
feat possible. Most of these modern appurte-
nances are toys which appeal to childlike people. When we sacrifice the adventure of trying
to maintain an inner moral integrity, we are
bound to seek for compensating thrills and to
find them in our mechanical toys.

But all this may be the voice of jealousy. I
love nothing so much in the realm of physical
pleasures as the sense of power which comes
from "stepping on the gas" when ensconsed in
a big car.

1928

Spoke today at the Jewish temple in ——. The more I make contact with the Jews the more I am impressed with the superior sensitiveness of the Jewish conscience in social problems. I have yet to find a Christian men's group that can surpass and few to equal the intelligent interest of a Hebrew group in the economic and social issues of the day. I do not say that there is not in privileged Jewish groups more moral complacency than is compatible with their avowed devotion to the Hebrew prophets, but there is at least a considerable appreciation of the genius of prophetic religion and some honest effort to apply the prophetic ideal to life.

I am afraid that the individualistic traditions of Protestantism, and perhaps also the strong Pauline strain in Protestant theology, have obscured the social implications of Jesus' gospel much more than is the case in Jewish religion. I am not sure that the religious life in the Jewish temple is always as obviously vital as it is in many Christian churches, but what there is of it seems to me to be directed much more astutely,

at least from the social viewpoint, than in our
groups.

The Jews are after all a messianic people, and
they have never escaped the influence of their
messianic, or if you will, their utopian dreams.
The glory of their religion is that they are really
not thinking so much of "salvation" as of a saved
society.

1928

The way Mrs. —— bears her pains and awaits her ultimate and certain dissolution with child-like faith and inner serenity is an achievement which philosophers might well envy. I declare that there is a quality in the lives of unschooled people, if they have made good use of the school of life and pain, which wins my admiration much more than anything you can find in effete circles. There is less of that whining rebellion against life's fortunes, less morbid introspection and more faith in the goodness of God. And that faith is, whatever the little cynics may say, really ultimate wisdom.

Mrs. —— has had a hard life, raised a large family under great difficulties, is revered by her children, respected by her friends, and she has learned to view the difficult future with quiet courage as she surveys the painful and yet happy past with sincere gratitude. She thanks me for praying with her and imagines that I am doing her a favor to come to see her. But I really come for selfish reasons—because I leave that home with a more radiant faith of my own. My confidence in both man and God is strengthened.

It is the quality in that woman's life that seems to me to be dissipated in the modern day, for all our progress. Perhaps we will work out something comparable to it some day in a highly disciplined culture. But as we lose the moral fibre of the generation of pioneers and wait for the discipline of a generation of moral aristocracy, it is ordained that we should wander through this present world where life is too comfortable to have the tragic nobility which our fathers had and too chaotic to disclose the charms which come from a great cultural and moral tradition.

1928

Here is a pastor singing himself to sleep. He writes: "Business men who attend church have sense enough to go out and run their business as Christians without the minister interfering with the technique. Many of the most spiritual and influential ministers I know never deal directly with politics, industry or reform." It is true of course that a minister can't offer expert advice on the detailed application of Christian principles to specific fields. But neither can he assume that principles get themselves automatically applied in the world's complexities.

One of the most fruitful sources of self-deception in the ministry is the proclamation of great ideals and principles without any clue to their relation to the controversial issues of the day. The minister feels very heroic in uttering the ideals because he knows that some rather dangerous immediate consequences are involved in their application. But he doesn't make the application clear, and those who hear his words are either unable to see the immediate issue involved or they are unconsciously grateful to the preacher for not belaboring a contemporaneous issue which they know to be involved but would rather not face.

I have myself too frequently avoided the specific application of general principles to controversial situations to be able to deny what really goes on in the mind of the preacher when he is doing this. I don't think I have always avoided it, and when I haven't I have invariably gotten into some difficulty. Nobody challenges principles.

Like the diplomats, the average man always accepts the gospel "in principle," and then proceeds to emasculate it by a thousand reservations. I know we can't be expert on every technical problem involved in modern industrial and national civilization. But the ministers who make a virtue of their pious generalities are either self-deceived or conscious deceivers.

1928

I am glad to hear of the new honors which have come to Bishop M——. He seems to me to be the most glorious figure in American church life. To have a philosopher, prophet and statesman all rolled into one, and to have that one achieve a peculiar eminence in our religious life is a clear illustration of how the richest character is achieved when various, seemingly incompatible, tendencies and functions are fused in one personality.

Philosophers are not usually prophets. They are too reasonable and circumspect to create or preserve the prophetic vision. The wise man is too capable of balancing the truth, to which he ought to be loyal, with some other truth with which it is in conflict. Thus he involves himself in the endless antinomies of intellectualism.

This philosopher is enough of a Christian to escape this fate. But he has another hazard to overcome; for he is a statesman. For years he has carried heavy responsibilities as a church leader; and it is always more difficult for a responsible leader, tied to an organization, to speak bravely than an irresponsible prophet.

Yet he has accomplished it. Here is a vindica-
tion of the power of the Christian life. Here is
a Thomas Aquinas and an Innocent III and
something of a Francis all under one hat. He
is not as much of an absolutist as Francis, of
course; and his power is not as great as that of
Innocent. But his learning would compare
favorably with that of Aquinas, and like the
great medieval philosopher, he has combined
the study of metaphysics with that of social
economy.

Strange that while I am so critical of bishops
my greatest hero should be a bishop and that,
while I call myself an anti-puritan, that hero
should be a Methodist bishop. So life defies our
prejudices and generalizations.

1928

I always thought I was a fairly brutal realist, but I am beginning to suspect that the whole thing is a pose to hide the sentimental preacher. At any rate now that the time has come to sever my connections with the church I find it almost impossible to take the step. There is nothing quite like the pastoral relationship. I would almost be willing to sacrifice the future for the sake of staying here and watching the lovely little kiddies grow up, and see the young boys and girls that I have confirmed blossoming into manhood and womanhood. There must be something bogus about me. Here I have been preaching the gospel for thirteen years and crying, "Woe unto you if all men speak well of you," and yet I leave without a serious controversy in the whole thirteen years.

It is almost impossible to be sane and Christian at the same time, and on the whole I have been more sane than Christian. I have said what I believe, but in my creed the divine madness of a gospel of love is qualified by considerations of moderation which I have called Aristotelian, but which an unfriendly critic might call oppor-

tunistic. I have made these qualifications because it seems to me that without them the
Christian ethic degenerates into asceticism and
becomes useless for any direction of the affairs
of a larger society.

I do not say that some one ought not to undertake an ascetic revolt against civilization.
Certainly there would be a peace in it which
no one can find who tries to adapt the principles of love to a civilization built upon the drive
of power and greed. Those of us who make
adjustments between the absolute ideal of our
devotion and the necessities of the immediate
situation lack peace, because we can never be
sure that we have our adjustment at the right
place.

Every moral position which has left the absolute basis is in danger of becoming a rationalization of some selfish purpose. I am not unconscious of the fact that my tendency to criticize
others so severely for their alleged rationaliza-
tions and hypocrisies springs from my own sense
of insecurity.

I persevere in the effort to combine the ethic
of Jesus with what might be called Greek caution because I see no great gain in ascetic experiments. I might claim for such a strategy the full
authority of the gospel except that it seems to
me more likely to avoid dishonesty if one admits

that the principle of love is not qualified in the gospel and that it must be qualified in other than the most intimate human associations. When one deals with the affairs of a civilization, one is trying to make the principle of love effective as far as possible, but one cannot escape the conclusion that society as such is brutal, and that the Christian principle may never be more than a leaven in it.

There has never been a time when I have not been really happy in the relationships of the parish ministry. The church can really be a community of love and can give one new confidence in the efficacy of the principles of brotherhood outside of the family relation. The questions and qualms of conscience arise when one measures the church in its relationships to society, particularly to the facts of modern industry. It is at this point where it seems to me that we had better admit failure than to claim any victory. The admission of failure may yet lead to some kind of triumph, while any premature confidence in the victory of a Christian ethic will merely obfuscate the conscience.

Modern industry, particularly American industry, is not Christian. The economic forces which move it are hardly qualified at a single point by really ethical considerations. If, while it is in the flush of its early triumphs, it may

seem impossible to bring it under the restraint
of moral law, it may strengthen faith to know
that life without law destroys itself. If the
church can do nothing else, it can bear witness
to the truth until such a day as bitter experience will force a recalcitrant civilization to
a humility which it does not now possess.

Reinhold Niebuhr

Reinhold Niebuhr is Vice-president of the faculty of Union Theological Seminary in New York City. Since 1928, he has been Professor of Christian Ethics and Philosophy of Religion at the Seminary. He was born in 1892 in Wright City, Missouri, where his father was an Evangelical Church pastor. After preparing for the ministry at Eden Theological Seminary in St. Louis, he studied at Yale, taking his B.D. degree in 1914 and his M.A. degree in 1915. After serving as pastor of a struggling church in Detroit (which, incidentally, provided the occasion for his writing the present work) he joined the faculty of Union Theological Seminary. Among his books are *An Interpretation of Christian Ethics, Moral Man and Immoral Society, The Nature and Destiny of Man, Faith and History, Christian Realism,* and *The Self and the Dramas of History.*